EASILY MANAGING GEN Z

Effective Communication Strategies to Unlock the Creative Potential and Balance Digital Distractions Within the Zoomer Workforce

DANIEL PAUL

CONTENTS

Part Three
OVERCOME FEARS AND EMBRACE INDIVIDUALITY

Part Four
MOBILIZE INNOVATION AND ADAPT TO CHANGE

INTRODUCTION

Legacy is not what I did for myself, it's what I'm doing for the next generation.

— VITOR BELFORT

Did you know that around 27% of Gen Z is expected to be a significant influence in the workforce by 2025? (Noor, 2023). Today, as many as five different generations, from Baby Boomers to Gen Z, are being combined in the workforce, and they all have different ways to express themselves and their ideas. I, myself, have experienced the integration of age gaps in the workforce, and I've observed how each generation brings unique skills, perspectives, and approaches to the team. It's fascinating to witness the growth of the work environment as I let people of different age groups collaborate. Gen Z, in particular, brings a fresh perspective to the workforce, as they are more integrated with technology. Accepting these youths in the workforce means you have to be ready for big changes in work environments in the future.

How exactly are they shaping the work environment? I've experienced firsthand the significant differences in how older and younger employees behave in the workplace. The elders value hierarchy, prioritize physical interactions over virtual ones, and may be a bit unfamiliar with digital tools. On the other hand, younger employees, especially Gen Z workers, are more adept at digital tools. They know how to communicate effectively in virtual rooms, often preferring digital communication, and they generally don't consider hierarchical status significant; in their eyes, a leader is not only the one in charge but also a guardian that they can rely on.

I've heard many complaints, from business leaders and managers alike, that Gen Zs are "difficult" to work with, that they are disobedient and lazy, and many others. Gen Zs are young and they are entering your team while they are still growing and learning. I think it's fair to say that most managers neglect the importance of mentorship and proper training for young employees. When Gen Z individuals enter the workforce, they are expected to possess a certain level of skill. However, this does not mean they can't continue learning and gaining new expertise. It is important to remember that everyone has the potential to grow when provided with the right opportunities. As a leader, it is your responsibility to create an environment that fosters learning. This is your time to improve your leadership skills to adapt to the ever-growing landscape of the 21st-century workforce.

You may have faced challenges as a manager of Gen Z employees, trying to keep up with evolving trends in the workplace or preparing for a leadership role in the team. In this book, I aim to guide you on how to understand Gen Z and their tendencies in the workplace. Starting from understanding their common characteristics and basic values to optimizing communication styles, this book will provide practical steps that you can implement in real situations to bring out the potential of the youngest generation in your workplace.

Gen Z, widely regarded as the first real digital natives, navigates a world in which connectivity is quick, knowledge is accessible, and change is the only constant. Understanding how they perceive work, interact with technology, and contribute to a collaborative environment is essential. You need to adapt to these in order to be a successful leader for the long term.

In this book, we will look at the numerous characteristics of Generation Z, including their employment expectations and the broader societal impact they have. As we peel back the layers, we'll discover the intersected relationship of technology and humans, the changing nature of connections, and how Gen Z's views affect workplace cultures.

By the end of reading this book, you will have an enhanced understanding of the Gen Z demographic and be knowledgeable about how to address their unique needs and provide mentorship to them. You will increase your leadership skills in many ways, not just in the area of communication. You will also learn more about integrating digital tools in the workplace, gaining new skills and insights that will lead to a more successful team.

Whether you want to know a little bit about Gen Z before accepting them in the workplace or you need to manage a multigenerational team, this book will prepare you for the future of the Gen Z-led workforce. Let your leadership shine by adapting to this generation's priorities and soon your organization will thrive by creating a supportive work environment for future generations.

WHAT YOU WILL LEARN

You will learn to manage Gen Z in the workplace using the Z.O.O.M framework:

- Z = **Z**ero in on Gen Z Characteristics
- O = **O**ptimize Communication for Clarity and Engagement
- O = **O**vercome Fears and Embrace Individuality
- M = **M**obilize Innovation and Adapt to Change

This framework doesn't only focus on isolated aspects of managing Gen Z but also on a holistic and sequential approach. You will begin with getting to know the Gen Z characteristics so that you can understand them better when they enter the workforce. Next, you will learn how to optimize communication, such as utilizing digital tools, visual storytelling, and creating a feedback loop system to increase Gen Z engagement in the workplace. Then, you will learn how to alleviate Gen Z's fears and embrace their unique individuality. The last step is learning how to mobilize innovation and adapt to the rapidly changing workforce dynamic.

This book is customized to adhere to Gen Z's unique needs. Featuring practical and actionable strategies, these methods are future-oriented, which will keep them relevant as your main leadership resource for managing Gen Z.

Are you ready to harness Gen Z's innovative energy and move your workplace forward? Join me on this exciting journey of discovery as we explore the complexities of Gen Z in the workplace and gain insights that will certainly affect the future of your team's success. Seize the opportunity to discover effective ways to manage this exciting generation while creating a collaborative workplace that supports their entrepreneurial spirit. Discover how to use their digital expertise and inclusive approach to promote positive changes inside your organization. Don't pass up this chance to adapt and succeed in the changing workplace landscape—arm yourself with the knowledge and skills required to effectively lead and engage with the lively Gen Z workforce. It is time to connect and empower the leaders of tomorrow!

Part One

ZERO IN ON GEN Z CHARACTERISTICS

Chapter One

UNDERSTANDING ZOOMERS—THE GEN Z PROFILE

Having grown up at a time in history marked by full digitalization, Gen Zs are the first true digital natives. They effectively navigate a world in which technology is a fundamental part of daily life, influencing their ideas and ways of communicating. With smartphones, social media, and immediate access to information at their fingertips, Gen Zs are skilled at multitasking and engaging with people all over the world. This exposure to a large digital landscape has enhanced their capacity to quickly adapt to new technology and drives their creativity to the furthest limit.

In terms of career and education, Gen Zs bring a distinct set of skills and expectations. They prefer interactive learning environments, and they use the internet to broaden their knowledge. They cherish flexibility, diversity, and purpose-driven work in the professional field. With these characteristics, adjustments to traditional employment frameworks may be necessary.

This transition in the workforce may result in communication gaps with older generations who are more familiar with traditional structures. In my experience, I find that Gen Zs typically prefer an inclusive work culture as they place a high value on open communication and feedback from supervisors and colleagues. This can occasionally clash with the hierarchal systems and more formal interactions in conventional workplaces.

As this generation steps into the workforce, they look for companies that share their values and respect their ethics. This shift in priorities may put traditional workforce values to the test, requiring companies to adjust to new expectations. In overcoming these obstacles, both Gen Z and older generations must collaborate to expand their expertise and creativity and form a common goal in the dynamic professional landscape.

To begin this chapter, I would like to provide a summary of the Gen Z profile, starting with their demographics, unique characteristics, basic values, and significant differences in their attitude to technology and communication methods.

WHO IS GENERATION Z?

Demographic Overview

Gen Z is a diverse and globalized generation born between the mid-1990s and the 2010s. Unlike its predecessors, this generation has grown up in an era where internet access has transcended geographical boundaries, influencing their view of various cultures.

They are nicknamed "Zoomers," as in the first generation to "zoom" in on the internet, emphasizing the importance of technology in their lives. They are also known as iGeneration, Net Gen, Centennials, Post-Millennials, or Homeland Generation.

Characteristics of Gen Z

Ethnically Diverse

According to census data from the US, Gen Z is the generation with the most ethnic diversity. Statistics prove that nearly three-quarters of Gen Zs in the 100 largest cities in the US belong to a minority group (The Annie E. Casey Foundation, 2011.)

Gen Zers are more likely to have grown up in a diverse setting, whether they grew up with immigrant parents, a single parent, in multiracial families, or in a household where gender and sexual orientations are mixed. As a result, they are more tolerant of variations of race, religion, and other differences than previous generations.

Digital Natives

Unlike Millennials, who grew up during the internet's revolutionary rise, the Zoomers were born into a world where cell phones, social media, and the internet were already prevalent. As the first real digital natives, Gen Zs have a natural comfort with digital platforms as well as the capacity to use technology for communication, learning, and social engagement. This technical fluency separates them from previous generations as they are much more adapted to the digital world and are able to utilize it effectively, on top of adapting better to new technological advancements.

This exposure to technology has a wide range of consequences for Gen Z. Their expertise with digital tools makes them quick learners, which is an important skill in a rapidly expanding technology. However, this exposure to digital devices has also been linked to decreased physical activity and increased sedentary behavior among Gen Z.

Pragmatic and Financially Minded

Having been through the aftermath of economic downturns, a global pandemic, and experiencing prior generations' financial struggles, Gen Zs have acquired a mindful approach to their finances. Unlike some myths that depict younger generations as financially careless, Gen Zs are aware of the significance of financial literacy and economic planning. The internet's ease of access to information has enabled them to educate themselves on personal finance, investments, and economic trends, making them more informed and strategic in their financial decisions.

When choosing careers, Gen Z individuals are more likely to value job security and financial stability. Many Gen Zers, with technology in their hands, have been finding new ways to produce income. When it comes to money, Gen Zs are one step ahead of millennials: they are the rising generation of digital entrepreneurs with a hustle culture. According to a Microsoft survey, around 22% of Gen Zers are juggling multiple jobs at once (Upton-Clark, 2023). This makes them particularly adept at money management and business.

Progressive

Gen Z tends to be more left-leaning. This political progression acknowledges the principles of social justice, equality, and environmental sustainability. Gen Z is defined by a heightened awareness of social issues and a desire to actively participate in positive changes. Growing up, the Zoomers witnessed movements such as Black Lives Matter, climate activism, the LGBTQ+ rights movement, and many more. Their progressive socio-political ideas distinguish them from previous generations as they passionately push for inclusivity.

Moreover, the existence of social media has heightened their awareness of societal issues. For them, social media is an excellent tool for voicing their thoughts and mobilizing like-minded people. Because of their ability to quickly exchange knowledge and organize online, Gen Zs are passionate about actively participating in political discourse and campaigning for topics that correspond with their views.

Educated

In comparison to most Millennials, Gen Zers' education displays a continued emphasis on higher education, with a higher likelihood of enrollment in college and university. Statistics show that 57% of Gen Zers in 2018 were enrolled in college (Parker & Igielnik, 2020). With our globalized work economy, Gen Zers recognize the importance of specialized skills and advanced degrees, which influences their desire for higher education. This generation understands the changing nature of employment and the need for constant learning, motivating an active commitment to education as a means of ensuring future chances. I do believe this generation's passion to find and learn new things is exceptionally valuable for the future of the workforce.

Mental Health Challenges

In contrast to their continual internet usage, Gen Z has been labeled the "loneliest generation." The impersonal nature of the internet and social media adds to their feelings of isolation. They are exposed to idealized representations of themselves and other people on social media. Furthermore, they are under pressure from academic and career expectations and face an uncertain future. These factors contribute to the rising stress levels among this generation.

Unlike previous generations, Gen Z's outlook on life is less positive, and they experience lower levels of social and emotional well-being. Despite being the generation with the highest social presence, Gen Zs frequently struggle with a lack of significant face-to-face interactions. The growing amount of screen time and virtual communication can lead to a disconnect from true, in-person interactions, therefore affecting their emotional well-being. This disconnect was exacerbated by the COVID-19 pandemic, and Gen Zers are facing the aftermath of this social isolation.

Shrewd Consumers

In terms of shopping, the internet has altered the landscape for these digital natives. The characteristics of the digital environment influence what they value when shopping. Gen Zs are more likely to pay for subscriptions, such as streaming platforms for music and movies rather than purchasing individual items. They also prefer to use subscription services for apparel brands, food shopping, and transportation. These services offer flexibility and the ability to try various products without committing to fixed purchases. This makes them able to explore their preferences and find products that are cost-effective, relevant, and personalized for their tastes.

Ease of access is important for this generation as they always prefer instant services and use their smartphones as an all-in-one device. Mobile payments, app-based services, e-commerce, and simple online transactions are Gen Z's favorites.

Gender Identity

In comparison to previous generations, Gen Z has had a significant shift in how they see gender identities and gender expressions. They exhibit more inclusive perspectives due to the fact that they most likely grew up in a more diverse environment. Gen Zs defy the binary conceptions, understanding that gender is a socio-cultural product, and it is more complicated than categorizing them into two separate boxes. This generation understands the importance of accepting diverse gender identities, which contributes to social inclusivity.

A survey says that nearly 60% of Gen Zers believe that there should be other options besides "man" or "woman" when being asked about gender (Geiger & Graf, 2019), and they are also more aware of terms such as "non-binary" and "gender-fluid." Their familiarity with a wide range of gender identities demonstrates a commitment to promote an inclusive society and detach themselves from traditional gender conventions. The acceptance of a larger range of gender identities by this generation will challenge harmful gender stereotypes and encourage a more nuanced understanding of various gender expressions.

Common Values of Gen Z

Diversity Is a Cause

From what I know of this generation's youth, the average Gen Z acquired a smartphone on their 12th birthday. This revolutionary technology has been with Gen Zs since they were young, and they may never know a world without the internet at their fingertips. The internet is the window through which these youths can navigate the world and learn that the world is much bigger than what is revolving around them.

Social media, in particular, has enabled them to connect with people from different backgrounds, creating significant cross-cultural exchanges. The ability of Gen Z to easily navigate this digital realm has led them to be a generation that welcomes variety as an integral part of their lives. As a result, Gen Zers are better prepared to welcome variety in all forms, from cultural and ethnic diversity to various gender identities, sexual orientations, and more. This cultivated mindset of valuing diversity from an early age will make a positive change for the future, in every aspect of life.

Environmentally Concerned

When it comes to environmental sustainability, Gen Zers are more concerned about this planet and they are willing to have a sustainable lifestyle. Climate change and environmental issues are one of their main concerns as they are growing up in an already concerning situation and are particularly worried about their future.

One of the most notable youth environmental activists, Greta Thunberg, is already fighting for eco-consciousness before she even hits her 20s. Despite all the mockery and criticism she faced, Greta stood by her values and carried on with her goals.

Her boldness in confronting world leaders and demanding immediate action on climate change shows that she takes responsibility and understands the long-term effects of environmental degradation. Her efforts also motivate other young people to become more conscious of their attitudes toward the environment. It's impressive how environmentally conscious Gen Zs are and how willing they are to speak up about it. I personally think that we, as the older generations, need to recognize what these youths are capable of and what positive impacts they will have on the future.

Ethical Consumption

Following their environmental consciousness, Gen Zers are also more ethical when it comes to buying items. A report by First Insight in 2019 stated that Gen Z shoppers care whether or not the products they buy are ethically sourced, and they are willing to pay more for sustainable products, more so than the previous generations.

This shift in consumer behavior is part of a larger trend toward more socially responsible and ecologically mindful actions. The preference for ethically sourced items among Gen Z will put pressure on companies to switch to sustainable methods and develop a market that values ethical standards. As this generation gains financial influence, their choices have the power to support a more environmentally friendly approach to consumption.

Mental Health and Self-Care

As Gen Zs begin to step out of lockdown after the pandemic, they are eager to reclaim their lost independence. There is no doubt that the events of the last few years have been extremely stressful for most Gen Z individuals, which is why they are beginning to recognize the value of mental health and self-care.

Gen Z is the generation of change and uncertainty. These complications contribute to their mental health, among other things such as education and career. However, unlike their predecessors, Gen Zs admit to struggling with emotional and mental well-being. One study shows that only around 15% of Gen Zs admit they have excellent mental health (Collins, 2023). This proves that they are fully conscious that the time-line they're living in needs a lot of mental resilience, but they don't sugarcoat it. They are authentic, honest, and more open about mental health, striving for a future that does not stigmatize mental health problems.

The openness of Gen Z about mental health issues, combined with their advocacy for destigmatization, will encourage people to start seeking professional help. Their willingness to openly discuss mental health can contribute to a more supportive and inclusive society, where people feel comfortable addressing their well-being needs.

Social Justice

There are a lot of social issues worth fighting for to promote a better future, and Gen Z is fighting for them. We need to start listening.

Gen Zs are passionate and idealistic youths as they have a lot of time ahead of them. As the first generation to be exposed to such high levels of crises—from environmental and economic to political—it is not surprising that most Gen Zs are more conscious about social issues. They are beginning to address social injustices, gender-based discrimination, racial justice, income inequality, mental health awareness, and many others. It is important that we realize the urgency of these issues and support the actions of younger generations as they will carry our future. Although Gen Z is a young generation, they have their own valuable perspectives, and they will have a big impact on future generations.

Individuality

Gen Zs are young and free, and they will embrace this freedom with individuality. The biggest myth surrounding this generation is that they are self-absorbed, narcissistic, and only think about themselves, but I've known many Zoomers in my life, and I believe that is not true. Indeed, they embrace an individualistic mindset—they want to be free in expressing themselves as people, are more self-appreciative, and hold their personal values to be an important part of their identity. However, they also enjoy connecting with people and are more likely to make a lot of friends, even if a lot of these friendships are maintained in the virtual world.

Gen Z is growing up in a world that values diversity and sincerity. This approach to self-expression is a desire to embrace the distinctive features that make each person unique. Their individualism is not a rejection of social principles, but rather a dynamic combination that improves society's structure.

Expressing ourselves confidently is one of many traits that I appreciate, especially in the workplace. Being able to be fully aware of yourselves and be confident about it makes you an interesting person, and I think we can learn these values from Gen Z.

THE SIGNIFICANCE OF TECHNOLOGY TO GEN Z

Gen Zs have 24/7 unlimited access to the internet and have been using it since childhood. Here are a few ways how technology has impacted this generation significantly.

They Integrate Physical and Digital Worlds

In this decade, online and offline activities blur together. We can talk to people online while shopping for groceries, have online meetings while doing the laundry, or read online news while eating—the possibilities are endless. Gen Zs have been incorporating this lifestyle since they were very young. To them, the physical and the digital worlds have little boundaries.

This trend doesn't stop at daily activities but continues in the realm of entertainment with video gaming, content creation, online streaming, and many more. With the help of technology, their physical appearance online might be different than how they appear in real life. The emergence of avatars, voice changers, animated face filters, or AI-generated images can completely alter how they present themselves virtually. It is impressive how fast technology has evolved and how proficient Gen Zs are at utilizing these new tools to create a completely different persona.

Mobile Tech and Social Media Are Used Daily

If you've ever wondered why youths these days can't seem to get away from their phones, it's because smartphones have been with them practically since elementary age. Smartphones are their lives—their whole personality— poured into one small item; it's no wonder why Gen Zs can't take their eyes off of them. They always want to know what's happening around the world; they want to be a part of it. They'll scroll social media for countless hours and live in the virtual world.

The same can also be said for other areas of their life, not just social media. They use e-commerce for shopping online, streaming platforms to watch movies and listen to music, and video calls to hang out with friends. They have become a generation that is very reliant on the internet, with the majority of Gen Zs (around 58%) admitting they can't go without internet access for four hours before becoming uncomfortable (Selig, 2023). Mobile technology is very important to them, and taking it away means taking away their lives.

Personalization and Privacy Become a Concern

With how fast technology is advancing these days, personal privacy is increasingly becoming a concern—not just for Gen Z, but for everyone. Gen Z in particular engages in the virtual world for hours on end, and I believe the awareness of possible privacy violations is more important than ever.

However, Gen Zs are quick learners, and with the myriad technological developments, Gen Zs might be the better ones to adapt faster to how they should share personal information online. This generation is more likely to question privacy settings, demand more transparent data regulations, and actively seek platforms that prioritize user safety.

Content Creation Becomes Popular

Content creators produce and share many digital creations—from videos, images, memes, blog posts, and many more—in a digital space. As the first generation to grow up entirely in the digital age, Gen Z is known for actively creating and consuming content in online places.

Content creation is driven by their desire to express themselves and connect with a wider audience. From my observation, it's clear that this generation has a lot of creativity and they are not afraid to show it. Thanks to easy access to a plethora of digital tools, platforms such as TikTok, Instagram, and YouTube are the keys to distributing their ideas, allowing them to be as unique as they want to be, and even develop online careers.

They Influence the Future of Technology

If you think that Gen Zs are the ones who adapt to technology, you'd be incorrect. In fact, it is the other way around. The tastes and preferences of these youths are what drive future technology to continuously adapt. We can take examples in the fields of telemedicine and online healthcare.

Even before the pandemic started, Gen Zs were already encouraging accessible healthcare everywhere, and that prompted the creation of new medical technology. Online health assistants, online health check-ups, and online consultations were all created due to the younger generations' dependencies on technology.

The same can be said for other areas as well: online education has become more relevant, workplaces started to implement remote working, food deliveries are quicker, and many more. It seems that their reliance on technology brings a lot of positive innovations.

They Are Global Thinkers

You'd be surprised at how most Gen Zers already possess more knowledge about other parts of the world than the older generations. They are encouraged to constantly explore other cultures, and even learn some things you may have never heard about. So, here is a little advice: don't be too skeptical or negative if a Gen Zer is telling you something that you don't know—you may learn something completely out of your radar.

The Pandemic Has Affected Their Digital Use

We've all experienced lockdowns, social distancing, and many health-related problems during the pandemic. Gen Zs, who were already dependent on digital use, are using it even more. Much like us, they need a place to connect, look for inspiration, and keep themselves busy. However, with Gen Z's creativity and their keen eye for improvement, these online activities are creating more communities.

Something that I have personally experienced working with Gen Zs is that when the pandemic started, they were the first ones to initiate mental health awareness and self-care. They encouraged other colleagues to start taking care of themselves emotionally and even proposed an idea to have online sessions where colleagues could freely share their problems. Their digital use, while sometimes concerning, is having a positive impact.

TECHNOLOGY AND GEN Z'S COMMUNICATION STYLE

Concise and Informal

Forget formal tonality and long paragraphs of emails when you're interacting with a Gen Z colleague. The average Gen Z colleague texts like this:

"Hi! Are you free tomorrow? Can we meet at 10?"

Gen Zs prefer short, concise, and informal communication. Despite the brevity, this communication style will encourage fast-paced interactions, which in turn makes them super efficient when working. Don't be scared to get friendly with your younger colleagues when texting. They like to use emojis to make the messages sound catchy.

Preference for Visual Media

Gen Zs prefer to communicate using visual media because it's more engaging and easier to consume. I can tell you that nearly half of Gen Zs prefer to hang out on platforms, such as YouTube, Snapchat, TikTok, or Instagram, that give them constant visual media. You can adapt to this style by focusing on pictures and videos in presentations to help Gen Zs understand you better.

Personalization

Experts say Gen Z prefers platforms that are easier to learn and use, adapted to their personal needs, and immersive to their experience. Gen Zs want to consume content that is relevant to their wants and needs, and the algorithm is already doing the job for them.

This personalization is important for Gen Zs as they want their needs to feel relevant. To adapt to this communication style, try to talk directly to them as "you" and "I" rather than using "we" or "us."

In-person Communication

Contrary to popular belief, Gen Zs prefer honest, intimate, and in-person communication. As an older generation, I thought that Gen Zs always go for video calls like Skype to meet their peers. However, Gen Zs always value honesty, especially from their supervisors. If you're managing a Gen Zer, don't be afraid to be close and personal with them. Invite them for a talk and give them honest feedback—they will appreciate it.

Social Responsibility and Transparency

Gen Z is known for leveraging social issues using social media. As such, they are not afraid to expose corporations and companies that may not align with positive ethical behaviors. This makes them appreciate transparency from the company they're working with. If they believe in your ethical practices, you will gain their trust. Try to be as honest and as transparent to your Gen Z employees as possible.

SUMMARY

Based on the discussion above, we can conclude that Gen Zs have different characteristics, values, and communication styles than older generations. Their proficiency with digital tools shows a distinct approach to communication and elevates them as leaders of change in our growing world.

As these digital natives advocate for social change and influence younger generations, I think it's important to know that they have their own values and communication styles. I'd like you to see these features as an increased diversity in the workplace rather than see them as communication barriers. In the next chapter, I will go into the depths of bridging the communication gaps between Gen Zs and older generations.

Part Two

OPTIMIZE COMMUNICATION FOR CLARITY AND ENGAGEMENT

Chapter Two

BRIDGING THE COMMUNICATION DIVIDE

Can you imagine a world where Boomers, Zoomers, Gen X, and Millennials all speak the same language and work together toward common goals? Well, if you can imagine it, then you can make it possible. Bridging the generational communication gap requires a collaborative effort to understand and appreciate everyone's distinct values and communication styles.

Now that you have learned Gen Z's unique characteristics, values, and communication styles, it's time for you to keep them in mind the next time you're interacting with a Gen Zer.

To start this step, I will discuss the differences in communication across generations, identifying the communication barriers, common misconceptions about Gen Z that can contribute to miscommunications, and strategies for team leaders in the workplace to communicate more effectively with Gen Zs.

IDENTIFYING COMMUNICATION DIFFERENCES

In this decade, as many as four different generations have entered the workforce, each of them bringing different communication styles to the table. Whether through a specific medium, frequency, or immediacy, different generations have to work with different preferences to achieve the same goal. This is why it's important to notice their preferred communication styles to avoid miscommunications.

Communication Styles Across Generations

Baby Boomers

Born between 1945 to 1964, Baby Boomers, also known as Boomers, emerged right after World War II ended when birth rates across the world spiked. This generation is accustomed to direct communication, minimizing digital use, since they didn't grow up with internet and social media use. Still, making telephone calls has impacted their communication preferences. Boomers are more comfortable with face-to-face communication and value the hierarchy structure in organizations. This means that they are more formal in professional settings.

Generation X

Gen X was born between 1965 and 1980. This is the time when people started to incorporate digital technology in professional settings, such as personal calls, emails, and faxes. As a Gen X myself, I find it comfortable to read formal and brief messages from colleagues. I also feel like I'm more accustomed to recent technology. So, it's easier for me to bridge the gap between the younger generations while at the same time being able to accommodate the communication style of Boomers.

Millennials

Most people in the Millennial generation have owned smartphones from a young age. It's no wonder that younger people are more adept at technology than I am, and I respect that. Because of this major shift in technology, I find that Millennials mainly prefer digital communications, such as texting, rather than phone calls.

According to a survey from Korn Ferry (2018), 55% of Millennials said that they are more comfortable communicating using text messages as answering phone calls is deemed "time-consuming." Therefore, the best way to connect with your Millennial employees is through online messaging apps, text messages, or emails.

Generation Z

Gen Z by far has the most distinct communication style in a professional setting. It can be challenging to adapt to this generation's communication style, with how fast technology is evolving these days. However, you must keep in mind that everything in their lives is quick and instant, and they expect fast responses as well. Hustle is their culture, and they will expect your prompt responses.

You must also note that Gen Z, despite being digital natives, prefers in-person communication. Try to combine these styles to match their needs: be concise, direct, honest, and friendly. It is also important to remember that they don't value hierarchy in organizations as much as older generations do.

Communication Barriers Between Generations

We know that different people born in different timelines are growing up in different situations. The different events they experience will shape them as a person. It can be difficult to relate to the younger generations if we aren't experiencing the world through their eyes.

I'm not telling you to completely immerse yourselves in younger people's lifestyles, but just knowing their differences will help you to interact with them. In order to achieve harmony across generations, we need to understand the communication barriers that may prevent common understanding.

Negative Perceptions and Stereotypes

There are lingering stereotypes about every generation. If we perpetuate this mindset, there will be no chance for harmony. You must break down these negative perceptions and see the younger generations as people who face their own challenges. Negative perceptions are one of many barriers that prevent generations from getting along.

During the years you were growing up, you faced generational problems of your own. For example, as a Gen X, I came of age when there was an AIDS epidemic and my parents were very strict about the friends I hung out with. On top of that, my family was heavily affected by economic recessions, which in turn impacted my adult life. College tuition was very expensive in the 80s, and we struggled to pay student loans. These are huge factors that have created my personality and mindset. Every generation has faced their problems and they've lived through them.

I have noticed the recent problems that Millennials and Gen Zs face nowadays, and I started to break down the negative perceptions I have about the younger generations: about how they are selfish, unfriendly, or impolite—these are all just misunderstandings. I guarantee you, that once you're able to let go of this negativity, you'll be better at befriending the youths.

Technological Proficiency

Gen Zs have more digital literacy than older generations. They are more able to quickly learn new user interfaces and navigate around the digital world. If you're working with a Gen Zer, don't be afraid to ask them how to use a certain digital tool. You need to eliminate the barriers that prevent you from learning new things just because you're reluctant to ask for help from a younger person.

Differing Values and Attitudes

Aside from technology, digital language is also evolving. In a technologically advanced society, the languages we use across generations are significantly different. For example, I notice that Gen Zs are able to smoothly communicate with their peers using pictures and memes. Moreover, they use a lot of abbreviations in texts that are practically unknown to older people, such as "iirc," "tbh," or "brb." These are confusing if you don't know what the words mean.

Their attitudes when socializing are affected by digital use and these languages. You may notice that younger people tend to be lighter in conversations, making jokes and showing their sense of humor, and some are even confident enough to directly converse with their supervisors. Remember that they value inclusivity in every form, so they're not so uptight when it comes to interacting with people of different positions. This attitude may come off as impolite or insensitive to older people, but I think it is important for everyone to feel comfortable in their own workspace.

Workplace Culture and Behavior

Different workplaces have different cultures. In my experience, an older, established company where employees are mostly of the older generations tends to value more hierarchy and mostly prefer formal conversations. In newer businesses, such as new start-up companies or online jobs, employees are more team-oriented and collaborative and interact on a daily basis like friends. These different workplace cultures may affect a Gen Zer if they enter a workplace that has a traditional culture. This can potentially create a barrier in which Gen Zs and older generations have difficulty understanding each other.

To overcome this barrier, you need to carefully observe how Gen Z employees behave with their colleagues. Surely, it's different than how older colleagues behave with each other. See these differences as a unique feature to promote their own work culture rather than seeing it as challenging traditional values.

HOW COMMON MISCONCEPTIONS ABOUT GEN Z CAN IMPACT WORKPLACE COMMUNICATION

Gen Z is the most misunderstood generation. According to a survey, around 74% of managers and business leaders think Gen Zs are more difficult to work with than other generations ("3 in 4 Managers," 2023). This number is unfortunate as I believe there's a big misunderstanding between generations.

If you belong to the older generation, your conceptions about Gen Z are most probably a stereotype or a generalization. You likely met a younger person who did not seem to value the olden days, and you automatically assumed that Gen Zs are all the same. I've experienced this firsthand while I was holding a meeting with colleagues. After the meeting was finished, a younger employee came up to me and suggested these points could just be sent through email or a text message without having to do a full meeting. At first, I thought that Gen Zs didn't value their leaders and never preferred physical interactions. However, after thinking through it, I realized that the materials indeed could be delivered through online messages so the team could work more efficiently.

There are a lot of misconceptions about this generation, and I think it's time we debunk them. These common misconceptions can negatively impact workplace culture and communication between colleagues.

Disloyal and Uncommitted

Gen Zs are young people who are passionate about what they do and they want their work to be meaningful. Once they've chosen a path, I don't doubt that they're going to use the opportunity as best as they can. If you think that Gen Zs can't be loyal to your organization, think again; they will follow organizations that respect their ethics. If they chose your team to work with, they chose it for a good reason. They are a purpose-driven generation, and they will stay loyal to their own values. This, in turn, will make them loyal to the company they're working for—as long as it aligns with their goals.

Stereotypes that all Gen Zs are disloyal and uncommitted can be potentially harmful to their work performance. If you don't trust that they take their responsibilities seriously, conflicts can happen.

Needy

If you're working with a Gen Zer, you probably think that their demands in the workplace— such as more diversity, inclusivity, career mobility, or time flexibility—might be too outlandish. However, I think that these requests are important for all employees. You may have never heard these requests from older generations before, but that's because Gen Zs are more aware of issues where inequalities are happening in society. They want to make sure that the workplace is comfortable, cares for everyone's well-being, and respects them as people.

Try not to see these requests as Gen Zs being needy; instead, view them as workers who value work-life balance. This misunderstanding can easily escalate into mismatched expectations in the workplace.

Lack Interpersonal Skills to Build Relationships

The average Gen Zer spends more time on their smartphone than going outside skateboarding with their friends. However, it's a big misconception that Gen Zs can't make friends. Remember that interactions nowadays aren't limited to only physical ones. I don't doubt that the average Gen Zer might have more friends than I do. They can connect with people from different continents, make friends in a social setting they belong in, and probably make friends from a video game community. Their connections aren't limited by distance.

They spend a lot of time online, but that doesn't mean they've forgotten how to communicate. Their communication style might change, but they still know how to build relationships in their own way. This assumption that they can't make friends will lead to an increased barrier between generations. We don't want to create a bigger communication gap between generations.

Lack Discipline

Maybe you thought that technology has made everything easier nowadays and that Gen Zs grew up lazy and undisciplined. They didn't need to get up at 6 a.m. and commute to work every day, and they didn't need to type paragraphs of emails to their supervisors. However, I want you to understand that while technology does make our daily activities easier, it doesn't necessarily create a weaker work ethic. We just need to adapt to the shift in this cultural progression.

Gen Zs are growing up in a highly competitive, digital environment. With how much younger generations are more career-oriented nowadays, Gen Zs have to fight for a position. Moreover, with how challenging the state of the economy is these days, they will have developed financial awareness, which in turn will give them a solid purpose in their career. In my experience, if they lack discipline, there's a good chance they weren't given worthy material to work on or they are doing something that they're not interested in.

If this issue is not communicated, it can potentially create an uneasy work environment where a Gen Z employee is not comfortable with the work they're given. Trust me, they can be just as disciplined as any generation—just make sure you give them something they're passionate about to increase their work performance.

Selfish and Entitled

Gen Zs are growing up in a fast-paced environment where everything is instant. Transportation services like Uber can drive them from one location to another without having to wait for a taxi. The same can be said for food deliveries, social media content, and worldwide news. Because of these instant gratifications, Gen Zs are deemed to be entitled and want everything to be handed to them on a silver platter.

I've witnessed firsthand how some Gen Z employees are willing to work extra time if what they are working on aligns with their goals. They need to know that their contributions will make an impact, both for themselves and for everyone else around them. So, if you want your Gen Z employees to work effectively, give them a clear purpose, make them understand your visions, and trust in their work ethic. An unclear objective will just confuse them, and this issue can negatively impact work culture.

Always Avoiding Physical Interaction

While it's true that most Gen Zs may not develop communication skills as early as older colleagues, it is not true that all of them don't value physical interactions. Understandably, Gen Zs are growing up with high digital use after the pandemic affected the way they interact, minimizing face-to-face communications. This may influence them to be particularly unaccustomed to confrontational situations. However, I don't believe that this makes them worse in terms of communication. They just bring different flavors, and there's nothing wrong with that.

Much like any generation does, they still need physical interactions from time to time. We are all social beings, and as much as Gen Z likes to surf the web, they still want to feel relevant in a professional setting. Be sure to check in on them every once in a while and ask for a team meeting should you feel the need to.

Communication styles differ for everyone as well. In this case, I'd suggest you ask which kind of communication is suitable for them. If this is not clearly discussed, it could potentially create ineffective communication between colleagues.

Can Answer All Tech Questions

Believe it or not, sometimes Gen Zs can be just as confused as we are when it comes to technical stuff. Assuming that all of them are experts in technology is going to create misunderstandings. Gen Zs are just like us: learning, developing, and adapting. They're fantastic with technology, but they're not experts at everything.

When engaging with a Gen Z employee, try your best to avoid stereotypes and assumptions. You need to get to know them individually and acknowledge what unique skills they bring to the team. If you assume that all Gen Zs are adept at every technical problem, you're potentially putting them under pressure, which may impact their work performance and create misunderstandings about how they want to operate in the workplace.

STRATEGIES TO CREATE A COMFORTABLE WORK ENVIRONMENT FOR GEN Z EMPLOYEES AND OTHERS

If you're a team manager or a business leader, you should have a common purpose to achieve a conducive and comfortable work environment with employees of all generations. Here are a few strategies on how to foster a work environment where Gen Z employees can communicate well with their older colleagues.

Increase Information-Sharing

In my work environment, I like to involve everyone in important projects, including the younger employees. I don't think that just because Gen Zs are younger than the rest of my colleagues I have to exclude them from certain projects. Their knowledge in certain areas, especially technology, will be beneficial for my team. I like to be transparent with them about information, share what they need to know, and believe in their competence. Perhaps you can implement this transparency with your Gen Z employees too. This increases their trust in your work ethic, creating an inclusive workspace where everyone can collaborate, regardless of age.

Show Career Progression

According to a qualitative study by Urick et al. (2016), the most concerning problem for younger generations in the workforce is the lack of mentorship and guidance from their older colleagues. The age gap and negative perceptions about one generation to the other is one of the roots of this problem. If you want to create a work environment where everyone can communicate effectively, you have to encourage career growth by giving guidance, especially to the younger employees. This can motivate them to value continuous learning and give them a fresh perspective in a certain field.

Explain How Individual Contributions Matter

When I recognize Gen Z employees' diverse skills and perspectives, I can better manage and work with them. You can also implement this in your workplace by making them feel included and that they belong in the environment. This will encourage further cross-generational communication and increase their engagement even more. If their individual contributions are valued, they will be more eager to collaborate with older colleagues.

Provide Specific, Constructive Feedback

Everyone loves feedback, especially Gen Zs. I don't hold back when I want to give them specific feedback on what they should improve in their work. This clearly communicates your expectations to them, and they will value the transparency from explicit guidance. Similarly, you should also encourage the older generations in the workplace to provide the Gen Z employees with specific feedback.

Harness Community and Connection

Connections that are delivered with empathy and respect will build trust among employees. This is particularly important in an intergenerational setting. Honest communication between generations is more likely to be effective. Gen Zs often desire mentorship, and older generations want to seek mutual understanding. By harnessing the importance of connection, employees will be able to find common ground.

Prioritize Wellness and Mental Health

I'd like to be aware of my employees' wellness and mental health—not just the Gen Z employees but everyone. Prioritizing emotional well-being will reduce the stigma around mental health problems—something that Gen Zs are particularly knowledgeable about.

In my workplace, I try to offer flexible work arrangements and encourage open communication about mental health challenges. Other methods such as providing mental health resources, training on mental health awareness, and promoting a healthy work-life balance can also be done. This will create a work environment that is supportive and beneficial for employees of all generations.

Understand and Respect Generational Differences

We need to recognize the differences between generations and how they contribute to the work environment. If we are aware of what each generation's cultural upbringing and their characteristics are like, we can easily bridge the communication gap. Each generation may have distinct communication preferences, and as a team leader, we have to respect them. Creating a work environment where each generation can communicate effectively allows for an inclusive and multi-generational work culture.

Foster a Supportive Environment

Lastly, as a team leader, promoting a supportive work environment is important if I want employees of all generations to work together. I try to lead my younger employees by demonstrating that I am empathetic and approachable. I always encourage everyone to openly seek help when they need it. In addition, I always put an emphasis on inclusivity. Regardless of age, all employees need to feel valued and included in the team.

SUMMARY

After discussing the common misconceptions and stereotypes about Gen Z, it's time for you, as a team leader or a manager, to slowly unlearn them. Gen Zs are the most misunderstood generation as of late, and I understand why. Their distinct ways of communicating and their demands in the workplace are fairly different from their older colleagues. However, implementing a supportive and inclusive work culture that appreciates generational differences can make a comfortable space for employees of all generations.

In the next chapter, I will encourage you to start learning about how to practice clarity and engagement with your Gen Z employees through the use visual communication.

Chapter Three

MAKING YOUR POINT—CLARITY AND VISUALS

A picture may be worth a thousand words, and this is especially true for on Gen Z. If you've ever wondered why infographics, ad campaigns, and media nowadays are more focused on visual styles, that's because companies want to stay relevant to this generation's preferences. Gen Zs are growing up in an era saturated with visual content, and they have developed an enjoyment for visual communication. I've seen this happen with how fond younger generations are of sharing images, videos, and memes with their peers, sometimes even providing information with a meme-based format where the audience can simultaneously laugh and understand the information being articulated.

In the workplace, this communication style can be harnessed to enhance your communication with Gen Z employees. You can study their trends and what visual format is relevant. Utilizing visual aids, infographics, and multimedia presentations will easily capture Gen Z's attention, while at the same time facilitating a clearer transmission of communication to them.

In this chapter, I want to guide you on how to incorporate visually engaging elements for Gen Z employees. This communication practice can better align your message with the digital and visually-oriented nature of Gen Z youths.

THE POWER OF BREVITY

"Brevity is the soul of wit," quoted Shakespeare in Hamlet. I think this is also true in the workplace. Being brief with your employees is a sign that you appreciate their time, while at the same time demonstrating that you're completely knowledgeable about the topics you're presenting.

You want to be efficient with timing to avoid employee burnout and to make sure they can digest everything. With Gen Zs in particular, time is money. Everything needs to be quick and instant, much like their lifestyle. If you want to communicate effectively with Gen Z employees, make sure to be concise and direct.

Crafting Concise Messages

This might need a little bit of practice. At first, I struggled to craft messages as concisely as possible without risking my important points not being made. However, upon further inspection, I can see how long messages can bore a Gen Zer even in the first sentence. For example, if I want to interact with a Gen Z employee, I don't want to send them messages like "Dear esteemed and valued employee;" instead, I would directly go to a brief greeting and address them by their name.

The same thing goes for making your purposes clear. If you want to invite them for an upcoming meeting, state the time and place. For example, your message could go like this:

> Hello, Maria. We will be having a team meeting at 3
> p.m. next Monday at the office.

Be specific, define the purpose, and personalize the message. By using their name, you're giving the impression that this is a personalized message and that you care for their contribution. Also, don't hesitate to use emojis or use a more informal tone. Gen Z employees will be more relaxed in communicating when their colleagues are laid-back and friendly.

Use Appropriate Communication Channels

Whether through a text message, email, face-to-face meeting, or voicemail, remember to choose the relevant channel to communicate. Different channels can work effectively for different types of communications. For example, if I want to discuss complex, sensitive, or confidential agendas, I would rather have a face-to-face meeting than go through text messages. Additionally, this type of meeting can be effective if I want to gather immediate responses from colleagues. On the other hand, if I want to share more detailed, important data and provide status updates, I would use email. Try to filter out which communication channels are relevant for the type of message you would like to send.

Encourage Two-Way Communication

Are you tired of Gen Z employees leaving you on read? The next thing you want to do is to encourage two-way communication. The only way to make them do this comfortably is to ask questions yourself.

I don't like when communication only happens one way. As a manager, I need to be proactive when it comes to engaging with employees. I don't always rely on Gen Zs to reach out to me when they need assistance, but I occasionally ask them to give me suggestions. For example, after a meeting, I would ask a Gen Z employee about what they thought about the meeting. Was the time spent effective? What else needed to be improved for the next meeting? This is a way to get them engaged with the workplace and gives them the impression that their opinions matter.

Use Storytelling

Aside from incorporating informal tones, you can try using storytelling to make Gen Z employees understand you better. When using storytelling, make sure to make it sound relatable and simple. For example, if you want to emphasize the importance of quality work over quantity, you could tell the following story:

> Do you remember that one classmate in high school who always finished their exams first? Meanwhile, you were still refining your answers to the third question. When I was in school, I felt that I couldn't be as efficient as that friend. However, once the scores actually came out, I almost always scored higher than the classmate who submitted first. In this workplace, I always appreciate quality work over quantity. Take as much time as you need and try not to submit rushed work.

You can adapt this story according to what your employees need.

Utilize Visuals

To relate with Gen Z employees better, I always prefer to do a presentation by focusing on visual styles such as infographics, icons, or symbols. Recently, I've been adopting the use of an interactive element, such as quizzes. When using quizzes, I try not to make it into an anxiety-inducing pop quiz. Rather, I would use simple trivia questions which I will explain in detail later.

A Gen Z employee recently suggested to me that I could use memes and GIFs in my presentations, which would make meetings more fun and engaging. You can try these presentation methods in your next meeting.

Establish Guidelines

There's nothing more uncomfortable in the work environment than unclear communication guidelines. To make sure that communications are clear for everyone, I always inform employees about work hours and through which medium we should communicate. I also encourage employees to inform me of their work hours so I can expect a prompt response based on the established time.

With this, I also implement more online communication with work-focused communication channels in chat-based platforms such as Slack or Discord. Ensure that employees have access to these tools and encourage them to contribute to the team.

LEVERAGING VISUAL COMMUNICATION

Visual communication is considered universal communication. If you can implement this type of communication properly, you will have your team understand your points easier. This will not only increase the engagement of the team but also cost you less time in trying to express your ideas. In this section, I will show you the essential knowledge needed to implement visual communication in the workplace.

What Is Visual Communication?

Using Visual Elements to Convey Ideas

Visual communication relies heavily on visual elements. In other words, the visuals are going to be the main carriers for your messages. It's worth noting that visual communication is an in-depth field of its own, and I recommend you seek counsel from colleagues who are more experienced in this area of expertise to help you with future engagements with younger employees.

In using visual communication, your main goal will be to communicate ideas in a clear, precise, concise, and engaging way. So, avoid using walls of text in your presentations. Typically, you would only need one to two catchy sentences, then follow the rest with visuals, while verbally expressing the ideas clearly.

Visual Communication Is Effective

Why is visual communication being used so much nowadays? Media has evolved a long way since its conception. We can now present images and videos digitally, with practically no cost. Visual communication is also connected with how the human brain works. Humans have evolved to be visual beings, where we practically process visual signals better than reading texts. This is due to the fact that the brain recognizes text as individual images that must be processed, thus resulting in longer processing time.

Compare that with looking at an image or a short video. We will register what it's about in a matter of seconds, without having to shift our eyes from left to right, reading a string of sentences. This makes visual communication particularly effective in the workplace as it saves a lot of time.

Makes Messages More Engaging and Attractive

Are your Gen Z employees tired of reading pages of reports like weekly newspapers? Trust me, using visuals in your communication will help tremendously with team engagement, especially for Gen Zs.

Aside from being quickly processed, visuals provide your audience with a variety of colors and movements, which are attractive to the eyes. When the team's focus is attracted to the discussion, they will want to engage further.

Versatile and Effective

People tend to memorize images better than texts, giving your messages a long-lasting impact. Remember that visuals are a universal language, and well-designed graphics are able to lower the barriers to communication. You can engage both Gen Z and older employees with the versatility of visual communication. You can be as professional, informal, or as humorous as you want—and everyone will still understand your point.

How to Use Visuals to Enhance Gen Z Communication in the Workplace

Utilize Digital Tools

Digital tools are your best friends when it comes to creating visually engaging presentations. Nowadays, we can utilize many digital platforms to create catchy, creative, and attractive presentations, and they are so easy to use. As Gen Zs become more prevalent in the workforce, I suggest you start familiarizing yourself with online digital tools, such as Canva or Powtoon. Not only will they ease your efforts in creating presentations but using these tools also gives you the impression that the workplace is keeping up with recent trends, which attracts more younger employees.

Promote Company Events Visually

When you have upcoming company events, use visual promotions such as leaflets or posters. You can also design the posters to match social media templates, for example in Instagram, where the media is heavily reliant on images.

Tailor Messages to Gen Z Preferences

Gen Zs know their way around mobile phones. When crafting messages, it's best to prioritize digital messaging. Ensure that the visual content they're consuming is mobile-friendly for optimized responsiveness. Gen Zs want content that is easy to access on the go. Additionally, you can also use interactive polls or quizzes to get them more involved.

Use Infographics and Diagrams

Infographics and diagrams are a great way to present complex ideas visually. You can incorporate bar charts, pie graphs, icons, and visually appealing colors. Recently, I've also tried using storyboarding when explaining step-by-step processes and project timelines. This method is essentially like creating simplified story progressions much like in comic books.

Incorporating Data Visualization

In emails, reports, onboarding, marketing, and branding, try to incorporate as many data visuals as you can. The most commonly used method nowadays is to make catchy company websites. Infuse interactive elements and show off your company profile using brochures and animated intros. This dynamic approach easily captivates employees and newcomers.

TECHNIQUES FOR VISUAL STORYTELLING

Why Visual Storytelling?

Visual storytelling is a simple strategy to convey ideas, evoke emotions, and captivate your audience. It places people and human experiences at the forefront, providing a personalized and empathetic approach to the audience. In many advertisements I've seen, storytelling strategies have been used to easily hook my curiosity. For example, advertisements for hair care products usually show a character who is struggling with real-life problems, such as having persistent dandruff. By giving the audience a relatable story, expressing ideas becomes much easier.

In this section, I want to guide you on how to utilize visual storytelling properly and why it helps with communication in the workplace, especially for Gen Z employees.

Reducing the Risk of Information Overload

Information overload is a real thing in the workplace, and Gen Zs are especially prone to it because it's their nature to access instant information from social media. From phone notifications to workload and online conferences, Gen Zs are deeply engaged with the digital realm. To avoid overloading information to your Gen Z employees, sharing information through storytelling helps to entertain them and keeps them away from the mundane for a while.

Makes Complex Information More Accessible and Engaging

It's not uncommon for complex information to be presented with visual media nowadays. As Gen Zs become more accustomed to digital communication, they have adapted to digesting information through visual presentations. For example, during the COVID-19 pandemic, visual storytelling of how the virus spreads and its effects was everywhere. Not only did the storytelling techniques promote collective understanding for citizens but it was also accessible to everyone, from public places to social media posts. Expressing complex information about a global pandemic would surely not be viable by using a bunch of text on a screen.

Creates an Emotional Connection

When you're using storytelling, you create characters and story progressions. Much like how audiences are captivated by movies or comic books, visual storytelling in presentations works the same. You are trying to emotionally connect the audience with information, creating stories that they want to follow. When the audience understands the story, it's easier for them to absorb information.

Can Be Used to Persuade and Motivate

Visuals can leave strong impressions, and creating a message can potentially influence someone to do something. The most prominent example I could think of is a food or beverage advertisement. The snappy storytelling style usually depicts a character eating a certain meal that quenches their hunger. It might be hyperbolic, but the storytelling techniques are effective in motivating someone to start buying the products.

Can Cater to Different Learning Styles

In the workplace, different people will have various learning styles. There are some people who are more adept at digesting visual information than text-based ones. Likewise, there might be people who prefer visual learning to auditory learning. However, in my experience, when incorporating visual storytelling in presentations, nearly everyone will get the point, regardless of their preferred learning style. This is what's special about utilizing visual storytelling in the workplace—it is engaging enough for your audience to be involved.

Ways to do Visual Storytelling

Show, Don't Tell

This is basic advice given to any storyteller. When you want to tell a story, don't spoon-feed your audience with every bit of information. Instead, let the picture do the talking. This technique of "showing" and letting the audience make interpretations of it for themselves will captivate their attention in no time.

Portray Dynamic Movement

GIFs, videos, dynamic photography, and animations play a big role in visual storytelling. You can use these mediums to your advantage. Other effects such as transitions, slideshows, and motion graphics are also valuable in your visual story-telling techniques. Dynamic movements in presentations will always attract the audience's attention, and with great transitions, they will follow the progressions better.

Tell a Whole Story

All the best stories begin with an introduction, introduce conflict, and have an ending. This is a familiar structure that I'm sure most of your employees will understand. If you want to present a story, you can start with a case study. Make up a name for the main character, describe their struggles and their journey, and then end with how they overcame their problems.

Remember Visual Hierarchy

Human eyes can focus on many things, but they particularly focus on bigger objects. When using visual storytelling, make sure you have your main point: the big elephant in the room. Once you've identified this, decide how you want to present the information and establish it as the focal point, usually at the center of the board. Make it contrast with the other visual elements and use a bright color.

Use Color Psychology

Color selections matter and good storytellers use color theory to its full potential. Keep in mind that I'm not saying you need to know the complex theories surrounding colors, but knowing which colors work together and which do not can be handy when creating visual presentations. For example, a yellow background won't look good when trying to present images because the brightness easily drowns images, which should be the focal point. Neutral or pastel colors such as white or cream work the best.

Some colors also have their own associated meanings. For example, the spectrum of red colors usually represents bravery, passion, or danger, while blue usually represents gloom and serenity.

Use Visual Metaphors

Like colors, images have meanings on their own. You can use images, icons, or symbols to describe some ideas. For example, using images of a house implies feelings of comfort and belonging; using images of a clock implies the passing of time, maybe that a deadline is getting close or a project is close to finishing. This technique also corresponds to the "show, don't tell" technique, letting your audience make meanings on their own without you explicitly showing every bit of information.

End With Your Strongest Image

First impressions are important, but so is the final image. Summarize the main point with a strong impact, such as a call to action, or circle back to the beginning of the story and how the change has been significant. Emotionally connect the story with your audience by using a quote.

RECOMMENDED APPS FOR CREATING VISUALS

Adobe Spark	One of the most prevalent software apps developed by Adobe Inc. It's targeted towards individuals with no extensive design experience but is still comprehensive enough to provide visually appealing content. Adobe Spark's specialty lies in its designs for creating social media posts and presentations, making it effective for digital marketing.
Canva	Canva is one of the most popular platforms among younger people as it provides a simple user interface. Canva offers countless presentation templates, brochure or leaflet designs, posters, and many more. It lets you make visually appealing designs with a pre-made format. Aside from templates, Canva also offers other design elements, such as images, graphics, and texts that are available to be modified.
Piktochart	Piktochart is a tool that lets users create infographics, posters, presentations, reports, and other visual content without the need for advanced design skills. Piktochart also offers free tutorial videos, blogs, resources, and how-to guides that help new users learn how to use the platform.
Visme	The extensive template library and its diverse features make Visme one of the most widely used digital tools in the workplace. Visme allows users to create interactive content, clickable infographics, and animated presentations. The platform also enables users to utilize teamwork, where team members can work simultaneously on one project.
Venngage	This online tool is specifically designed for creating infographics and data visualizations. Users can choose from a wide range of templates, such as statistical, step-by-step processes, and many more.
Google Drawings	This online tool is a web-based diagramming and graphic design tool and is part of Google Workspace. This online tool integrates with other Google applications such as Google Sheets and Google Docs, which makes it easier for workers who rely on Google Workspace tools. It's also free for anyone with a Google account.
Microsoft PowerPoint	This is one of the most used presentation softwares being a part of the Microsoft Office suite. PowerPoint is known for its user-friendly interface that is easy to learn, making it an easy option for workplaces with multigenerational employees.

Adobe Creative Cloud	This software is suitable for professional designers, videographers, photographers, and other visual artists. Adobe Creative Cloud offers users a wide range of tools for designing. This is a comprehensive software, and it is recommended for users with extensive knowledge of visual design.
CorelDraw Graphics Suite	CorelDraw is a popular software designed for graphic design and illustration. The app is known for its wide set of tools to facilitate creative tasks, from designing logos to digital art.
Esri ArcGIS StoryMaps	This is a web-based platform developed by Esri, a leading provider of Geographic Information System (GIS) technology. ArcGIS allows users to create multimedia-rich stories that can combine maps, data, and images. It's designed for spatial storytelling, incorporating geographic data into the design.
Shorthand	This is a platform to create visually appealing digital stories. It's specifically designed to create storytelling presentations by combining texts, images, videos, and other interactive elements.
Pixlr	Pixlr is an easy-to-use media editing app, and it is available on mobile phones. The simple user interface is suitable for younger users. The app is focused on quick and easy editing tools.
WeVideo	This is a video editing platform that is accessible to users of varying editing skills. It's cloud-based, meaning users don't need to install software on their devices but will have to rely on an internet connection. WeVideo has a green screen feature, voiceover recordings, and many more.
Camtasia	Camtasia is popular for its screen recording feature. This software is made for creating presentations, professional videos, and other screen-captured content. Camtasia provides a variety of annotation tools to emphasize specific points in the video and allows audiences to interact with the video.
Moovly	Moovly is a tool to create animated presentations, videos, and other multimedia content. It's super accessible and user-friendly. From video editing, animation, and presentation tools, Moovly has a comprehensive media library. It can also integrate with other platforms, such as YouTube and Vimeo.

From this chapter, you have learned how to practice effective communication using visualizations. Whether you're managing Gen Z employees or those of older generations, the topics that have been provided here are valuable in various settings. Remember, brevity is powerful, and it's time for you to effectively utilize this skill to achieve harmony with your employees.

In the next chapter, I will take effective communication to the next stage where we'll look at open dialogue and continuous feedback.

Chapter Four

OPEN DIALOGUE AND CONTINUOUS FEEDBACK

F eedback is the breakfast of champions and Gen Z craves it daily. I want to tell a story of the first time I managed a Gen Z employee. Unlike my older generations of employees, this Gen Z worker liked to take up most of my time just to ask what I thought of their daily progress. This happened almost daily. Every afternoon they would send me a screen capture or come to my desk and ask for direct feedback. This was undoubtedly a new situation for me, as I rarely had to provide so much open communication to older employees. The work was quite hectic and slow, but nonetheless accurate. They would only need to revise a few things before sending me the report, and I was impressed with the quality.

A feedback loop is crucial for these youths, and they won't hesitate to ask for help if they're stumped. If you think that they will be a hassle to deal with—having to openly communicate every day or two—you might need to focus on the later outcome. Would you rather receive quick work full of inaccuracies, which would need extra time and effort to fix, or work sent near the deadline, but having little to no need for revisions?

Personally, I would choose the latter, and I am more than available to guide my Gen Z workers toward open communication so they can work better in the future. If managers and team leaders aren't providing their employees with direct feedback, how can they improve? This is something that I've seen many Gen Zs struggling with in the workplace; they aren't being provided mentorship, and we rarely realize they're struggling with progress. The truth is, Gen Zs aren't lazy; they just need proper guidance. Trust me, most Gen Zs are quick learners; as long as you give them valuable and constructive criticism, they will try to push to their limits.

In this chapter, I want to guide you on how to foster a work culture that is accustomed to continuous feedback and open communication. By creating a culture where everyone—not only Gen Z employees—can freely share their insights and opinions with each other, you will set the stage for people to thrive and fulfill their meaningful purposes.

FOSTERING OPEN COMMUNICATION

Creating a Culture of Openness

Creating a work culture where feedback is integrated into daily interactions requires a proactive approach, and everyone must contribute to it. As a leader, you can start by setting an example, but it's important to acknowledge your multigenerational employees by recognizing the various spectrums of their ages and which timeline they grew up in. Let them introduce themselves individually, and welcome each to the team with open arms. Their ages may be different but their purpose stays the same, and I think that's what's important.

Encourage Open Conversations About Generational Differences

To start this, I like to ask the team about what their weekend routines usually consist of. Some will probably answer something like: wake up at 6 a.m., eat breakfast, get dressed, and then do some relaxing activities. Then, someone else would answer with waking up at 7 a.m., checking their cell phone, going for a jog, and so on. Notice how different people have different routines because they are different people with their own needs and motivations. When trying to encourage open conversations about generational differences, we must first recognize the smallest differences, as these differences are essential to one's life. This makes it easier to relate to each other, regardless of age.

Everyone can start recognizing their differences, such as the differences between routines. For example, older people might prioritize physical interactions with their families, while Gen Zs might prefer to continue working during weekends. This doesn't mean that generational differences can be easily grouped into boxes, but you may be able to observe some commonalities. For instance, I have noticed that younger individuals tend to be more inclined towards using their gadgets in their free time. This could be a key feature in recognizing generational differences and opening further conversations between generations.

Create Opportunities for Employees to Socialize Across Generations

Not everything has to be done working in front of a screen—you can encourage employees to socialize. To create these opportunities, you can try grouping different age groups together so that they can socialize with each other. I like to combine teams with different age groups to encourage inter-generational communication. I usually start with an easier pairing, such as Gen Zs with Millennials. They are both adept at technology and may socialize together naturally. This allows both sides to start learning about their generational differences and learn how to communicate effectively with each other in the workplace.

Provide Mentoring Programs

Mentoring is a valuable program that can help you to manage a multigenerational workforce. Here are some common mentoring styles:

- cross-cultural mentoring: This mentoring style combines employees from different cultures and backgrounds. This can help employees get to know each other's differing cultures and learn how to be more inclusive.
- reverse mentoring: This mentoring style combines experienced, older employees with promising Gen Z youths. Younger employees can provide insights into technological trends and how to use new gadgets, while older employees can provide wisdom and advice based on their work experience.
- intergenerational mentoring: this is a good way to get employees from different age groups to interact with

each other, whether through big groups, small groups, or individually. This can be especially helpful for employees with big age gaps, such as those from Gen X and Gen Z.

Respect the Unique Perspectives of Each Generation

Remember what I said about different weekend routines? Differences are essential in this life. While perspectives are different for each generation, they all have their purpose. In the workplace, different skills, experiences, and perspectives are valuable to encourage innovation. For example, in my team, a Gen Z employee introduced us to the easy drag-and-drop feature in digital tools like Canva. If we never took their knowledge of digital tools seriously, we would still be stuck using PowerPoint transitions, without knowing that there are much more diverse tools that can be used.

Offer Inclusive Benefits

In order to recognize the diverse needs, preferences, and values of a multigenerational workforce, you need to implement benefits that are inclusive and applicable to employees of all age groups. In my experience, offering flexible work arrangements, such as the option to work remotely, is popular for workers of each generation. Nowadays, workers value autonomy and flexibility, and this in turn encourages employees to improve their work-life balance.

Other than that, I find that health and wellness programs, such as mental health support, are beneficial for everyone. Most employees, regardless of age, are beginning to see the importance of keeping their mental well-being in check. Other inclusive benefits include family benefits, such as parental leave and childcare assistance, which are great options. Of course, you can adapt to your employees' needs by acknowledging their different priorities and planning the benefits accordingly.

Promote a Shared Sense of Purpose

It's not enough to just set goals for the team; you also need to involve everyone in the mission. When employees have a shared sense of purpose, they'll be better able to interact with each other since they know what they're trying to achieve together. Encourage employees of all ages to contribute their ideas and foster a sense of ownership in the mission. In other words, make the goals a combination of their perspectives. After this, don't forget to encourage everyone to celebrate achievements together.

Challenges You May Face in Encouraging Open Communication

Let's face it: embracing change while at the same time trying to cater to different needs simultaneously is going to be challenging. As leaders, we must be ready for the possible obstacles in the future. I have to admit, managing a multigenerational workforce will take a lot of trial and error, and you might need to change plans occasionally to keep everything organized. This is especially true if this is the first time you've managed Gen Zs in the workplace—there might be more adjustments needed.

In the following section, I want to share the potential difficulties team leaders and managers might need to face in trying to implement new systems in the workplace.

Different and Shifting Priorities

Different generations are going through different stages of their lives. Older employees might give more priority to their families and children, while younger employees might put their careers at the forefront. Some might still be in school, and some others could be caring for their elderly parents. Whichever the case, employees' priorities vary, and this is challenging to handle. Not only could this possibly divide each employee's core ideals, but it would also have an impact on their work performance if their needs were not fulfilled.

When creating a new communication system, you might find that you will need to adapt to the needs of different employees, and you can't simply integrate everyone's individual priorities. In this situation, one effective solution is to hand out a questionnaire or conduct a survey. Learn the different priorities your employees might have and try to find the most suitable common ground. Additionally, it would be better if you could check in on them once in a while to ensure that their needs are being met.

Mismatched Communication Styles

The most common problem leaders find in the workplace is acknowledging the different styles of communication. You may be tempted to use online group chats or video conferences to follow the popular communication style of Gen Zs; however, there may be some senior employees who could benefit from direct contact with supervisors. It would be unethical in this scenario to have a workplace communication style where there is only digital communication.

Additionally, some employees might work better in an individual, autonomous, and private setting, while others might prefer teamwork and collaboration. In this situation, I'd like to implement team assignment rotations. Task rotations would be beneficial for employees to experience diverse work settings, allowing them to both engage in independent and collaborative spaces.

Work-Life Balance Expectations

In the workplace, work-life balance is an intricate subject to touch. Balance is when something functions within a certain equilibrium, and achieving this balance is different for everyone. Some people define work-life balance as the ability to navigate both professional and personal lives without interference from the other. Some people define work-life balance as having an equal amount of time for work and personal life. Whichever the case, people have different expectations when it comes to having a work-life balance.

As a leader, you need to understand these personal expectations. There might be instances where an employee's personal life may interfere with their professional situation. In this case, I always like to be sympathetic to critical life events, such as family emergencies, or other personal problems, but it's important to encourage employees to set clear boundaries between their personal and professional lives.

Embracing Change and Innovation

Dealing with change is always uncomfortable in the beginning. However, whether we like it or not, improvement comes from innovations, and innovations are driven by change. As a multigenerational workforce, embracing change and innovation is crucial—improvements can't happen if the workplace isn't comfortable with change.

If your team consists of mostly older generations, change might be more challenging to face. In this situation, you also need to understand that changes don't happen overnight. What you need to do is slowly but surely implement the changes, such as more flexible work hours, offering a variety of digital communications, and so on. Don't rush the process, but still make sure that employees are gradually comfortable with the newer systems.

Stereotypes and Discrimination

No generation is without its own stereotypes—it's not just towards the Gen Zs. I've seen many younger workers often avoid working with Boomers because they're deemed "too uptight," "rigid," or "judgmental." On the other hand, Gen Zs are also often seen as disobedient and lazy. We know these stereotypes are mostly misunderstandings and generalizations, but they can lead to unpleasant interactions in the workplace, including discrimination.

In a multigenerational workplace, I like to implement a zero-tolerance policy, and this includes age discrimination. Regardless of age, everyone needs to be heard. As a leader, I also need to make sure everyone appreciates diversity, and this can be done by actively acknowledging the different cultural backgrounds of my employees.

PRACTICING ACTIVE LISTENING AND GIVING FEEDBACK

Active listening is a fundamental aspect of open communication and engagement. It involves giving full attention to the speaker and demonstrating empathy for what they are expressing.

In addition to active listening, giving feedback is just as important. If you want to give proper feedback, you have to properly listen to their requests. This gives both you and your employees an opportunity to understand each other. You will get insight into their strengths and which areas they need to improve, and they will learn how to be transparent and to trust you as a leader. All of this will lead to a chain of beneficial outcomes: building a positive, open, and honest work culture and providing a space for employees to freely express themselves without fear of judgment.

You might have heard about the importance of active listening, but have you practiced it properly? In the next section, I want to talk about how to be a leader who actively listens and gives constructive feedback. Are you a good listener? Let's find out.

Techniques for Effective Listening and Feedback

Active Listening Techniques

- Limit distractions.

While having a conversation or holding a meeting, eliminate distractions as much as you can. Turn off your mobile phones, only use gadgets that are necessary, close the office door, or be in a quiet space if you're holding an online meeting. Distracting noises will make interactions unpleasant, and this is especially true when you're trying to listen to your colleagues.

- Use the right body language.

Is there any "wrong" body language? Yes, if we're talking about a specific situation. I shouldn't openly yawn in front of an employee who is currently sharing their opinion. I should also avoid checking my watch or my phone when having a conversation. Body language is important, and this demonstrates how well you can give attention to the speaker. Constantly being distracted, not maintaining eye contact, or not being responsive are examples of bad body language, and you should pay attention to these.

- Focus on the present.

What should I eat for dinner? Where did I park my car? Random questions like these may occur in your head when having a conversation. While this may be inevitable, it is important to stay focused on what's happening in front of you. If possible, make sure you are in a focused head space before having the conversation.

- Listen to understand.

Don't just listen; listen to understand. You may have thousands of questions in your head as you listen through the conversation. However, when practicing active listening, try to set aside your personal opinions. You are trying to listen to someone else, not yourself. Understand the nuances of their opinions and try to look at the situation from their perspective; in doing this you might gain new ideas.

- Do not interrupt.

Whatever questions and opinions you have now, hold them for later. In this case, I usually like to bring a small notebook and write down a few questions that I might need to ask later. Active listening is paying attention to the speaker without interrupting their flow.

- Pay attention to non-verbal cues.

Aside from using the right body language, you can try paying attention to the speaker's non-verbal cues. Facial expressions, gestures, and tonality are little details that can enhance your understanding of them. Are they nervously shifting in their seat, rubbing their eyes as if tired, or have their arms crossed, upset? These gestures can tell you as much as words.

Feedback Techniques

- Embrace negative emotions.

Giving feedback can be uncomfortable, but this is also true for the receiver. When giving feedback, it's important to know that there might be some unpleasant emotions. Nervous, anxious, tense—these are emotions that you might feel when giving feedback, to name a few. On the other hand, receiving feedback can also invoke negative emotions, such as feeling embarrassed, insecure, overwhelmed, or demotivated.

As a leader, I believe it is my responsibility to create a comfortable environment for employees to receive feedback, and I should be aware of these potential negative emotions. You can communicate this clearly before the feedback session begins, to acknowledge that both parties may feel uncomfortable and that it is normal, and we should accept these emotions to be able to have effective communication.

- Be specific.

There's nothing more confusing than giving unclear feedback. If you're trying to give corrective feedback, be clear about what's lacking and what needs to be improved. If I said something like, "Your report yesterday wasn't very satisfactory, you need to do better," it would leave an employee confused and underappreciated. Instead of focusing on their mistakes, you can clearly state what seems to be the problem and ask if there is anything that can be done to alleviate the problem. For example:

> I noticed there seems to be a lack of active participation from you in our last two meetings. There were instances where your input would have been valuable, but you seemed to be hesitant in sharing your thoughts. Is there something that makes you reluctant to communicate with the team?

In the example above, I spoke clearly about a specific problem, acknowledged their position on the team, and asked about what could be done to address the issue. Specific feedback like this will inspire your employee to speak out and tackle their current challenges.

- Use empathy.

Empathy is a leader's biggest strength. When giving feedback, I always make sure to show them some empathy. Always use "I" remarks when trying to give feedback.

Recognize that they are people with their own problems, and demonstrating empathy will help to decrease negative feelings.

- Provide regular feedback.

Don't postpone feedback sessions, and don't limit them to only once a year. Do it regularly and consistently—frequent feedback will make a huge difference. The best leader knows when to provide regular employee feedback and sticks to a schedule.

- Keep it private.

Most of the time, I avoid public criticism. Most people just don't like public recognition, regardless of whether it is a negative or a positive critique. If I have something to say about their work, I'd rather do it privately. Trust me, private feedback sessions are always more effective as this prevents any unwanted public interactions and boosts employees' confidence.

- Avoid the sandwich approach.

Remember what I said about being specific with your feedback? Avoid using the sandwich approach, the type of feedback where you jump between negative and positive critiques, "sandwiching" your statements. You might be trying to soften the blow about their previous mistakes, but this could potentially confuse the employee. Be clear about your objectives: do you want to provide corrective feedback or encouraging statements? Focus on the issue you want to resolve and make your statements direct.

- Focus on performance, not personality.

Different working styles will create different results. I've noticed that certain creative employees approach their work inventively, at times straying from the original project. However, this doesn't mean that they perform poorly; they just need some guidance to be put back on track.

When providing feedback, make sure to focus on their performance rather than how their personality affects their work. An outgoing employee might perform better in teamwork collaboration, while others might prefer private work. These different personalities are just varieties in the workplace, and as leaders, we need to respect them.

- Follow up.

After giving feedback, make sure to monitor their progress by asking follow-up questions. This will ensure that your employee receives the feedback they need. Moreover, if they require further help, it's a great way to encourage them. Asking follow-up questions will also give them the impression that you care about their work performance and you appreciate their progress.

IMPLEMENTING A CONTINUOUS FEEDBACK LOOP

What Is a Feedback Loop?

A feedback loop is a continuous feedback system that allows for a regular exchange of ideas, comments, opinions, suggestions, and so on. It's an important system that keeps the line of communication open for the team. This is especially beneficial for Gen Z employees as their engagement with the rest of the team will create a daily exchange of creative ideas.

How to Do It?

- Collect feedback.

The first process is to actively seek input from team members. Use surveys, discussions, and team feedback sessions to gather insight into various aspects of the work environment.

- Analyze the collected feedback.

Once feedback has been collected, the next step is to collaboratively analyze the data. You can start by identifying recurring patterns or areas that require the most attention. Don't forget to look for strengths and what's needed for improvement.

- Use insights in decision-making.

The next step is integrating all the insights gained into strategic planning, project development, and further team management. Using team members' perspectives for decision-making will create an inclusive work culture that values the input of every individual.

- Create a loop of continuous improvement.

This is an ongoing process, hence the loop. After making decisions based on feedback, it's time to continue collecting insights on a regular basis. This continuous improvement loop, which affects decisions, becomes a repeated cycle. This process ensures that your team stays attentive to each other's changing needs and fosters a healthy work environment for everyone.

Involves Many People

One of the key strengths of implementing a feedback loop is its transparency. Your team will gain access to various viewpoints and experiences that make the team whole. This inclusivity will generate a sense of ownership among employees because they will be directly involved in the decision-making processes.

Appeals to Gen Z Workers

As we know, Gen Z workers appreciate transparency and continuous feedback, and the feedback loop system is perfectly in tune with these core values. Many Gen Zs are accustomed to constant interaction with their peers, and they expect to be heard. Companies may retain more fresh and promising young talent from Gen Z by implementing this feedback loop system.

Has Many Benefits

I believe that effective communication is the lifeblood of any successful business. The benefits of this feedback loop system are practical and tangible, ranging from improved communication to higher employee engagement. Regular feedback promotes a work culture that is easily adaptable, making companies remain flexible in the face of uncertainty. It also acts as a preventive strategy, addressing potential issues before they become critical.

SUMMARY

In this chapter, we have explored the transformative power of cultivating a work culture that values open communication and continuous feedback. The integration of a feedback loop mechanism allows a collaborative approach to problem-solving and team development. We've learned that these principles align well with the expectations of Gen Z workers, who appreciate transparency and constant feedback. Adopting this approach can result in increased employee engagement and improved team chemistry.

In the next chapter, I will guide you on how to build trust with Gen Z employees, putting honesty and clarity at the forefront to overcome Gen Z's potential fears in the workforce.

Part Three

OVERCOME FEARS AND EMBRACE INDIVIDUALITY

Chapter Five

HONESTY AND DIRECTNESS—BUILDING TRUST

I n the Gen Z world, honesty isn't just the best policy; it's the only policy. They believe in being honest to themselves and expect others to be as well. In a world full of filters, Gen Zs aspire to cut through the mess and enjoy true connections. They recognize that solid relationships are built on honesty. As a result, in their pursuit of authenticity, they hold themselves to the highest levels of honesty and integrity.

I recall a scene from the comedy TV show *30 Rock* in which actor Steve Buscemi tried to appeal to a group of high schoolers dressed youthfully while holding a skateboard, saying, "How do you do, fellow kids?" (Fey et al., 2012.) Most young people know this as a meme, but it is an interesting scene when trying to make a point about displaying authenticity, especially in a situation where older people have to blend in with younger people.

Steve Buscemi, who was 55 years old at the time, was out of touch with the rest of the environment. No matter how he tried to appear youthful, the teenagers weren't impressed;

they were confused instead—or what I believe Gen Zs would call "cringe." Furthermore, the fact that he referred to the teenagers as "fellow kids" indicated that he was unfamiliar with juvenile jargon; I'm sure teenagers wouldn't refer to their friends in that manner. While this was merely a scripted comedy show, it could happen in real life.

You may be tempted to learn how to communicate with slang like Gen Zs do with their peers, but I would advise against trying to memorize a whole new vocabulary in order to appeal to them in the workplace. Sure, you can look up new phrases in the urban dictionary, but trying to impress them will fall flat. As long as you're friendly and respectful, I'm sure Gen Zs will appreciate your existing vocabulary.

In this chapter, I want to guide you on how to practice transparency, authenticity, and honesty in the workplace. Interacting with Gen Z means being honest and true to yourself, without trying to impress them. As a Gen Z once told me, "You don't need to be like us if you're trying to appeal to us." Gen Zs appreciate authenticity, and they know the things that make you unique will make you stand out from the crowd.

THE IMPORTANCE OF TRANSPARENCY IN THE WORKPLACE

Transparency in the workplace is all about cultivating a culture of openness and accountability. Everyone will adapt how to communicate with colleagues, inform decisions and goals, as well as establish a culture in which everyone feels valued. In a transparent workplace, communication flows freely—no longer will decisions and changes be made only between leaders and supervisors. This will dissolve hierarchies in the workplace and promote a sense of shared responsibility. So, how is this system important in a multigenerational organization?

Fosters Trust Among Employees

I'd like to imagine employees can get information much like how they can get information from newspapers or social media. Information flows freely and doesn't require premium subscriptions to access it. This kind of culture will foster trust among team members, knowing that no information is hidden and decisions are not one-sided.

Improves Employee Engagement

Imagine if you were told to build a dam near where you live, but you weren't told what it's for. Would you feel the need to build it? Employees need a clear goal when given a project. When they understand the bigger picture and the collective goals, they will be more engaged in their work. This is where transparency becomes important. If you're aware that there will be a flood coming and the dam is meant to protect your neighborhood, you will feel the need to build it.

Breaks Down Innovation Barriers

Creativity is innovation's best friend. If you want your company to keep adapting to future advancements, you have to allow various ideas in the workplace. Gen Zs are great outlets for creativity and innovation. Being transparent will make employees more inclined to contribute their creativity as their perspectives and collaborations are valued. This free flow of ideas stimulates creativity, and you may never run out of new insights.

Attracts Better Candidates

What's more attractive to a Gen Z than the honest reputation of a company? Gen Zs are bright youths, and it would be a shame if their talents aren't put to good use because their workplace isn't accepting of innovative ideas from younger people. Gen Zs are looking for jobs that practice honest communication—not just between colleagues but with super-visors as well. Transparent communication will provide them with a pleasant applicant experience by demonstrating the company's principles from the start.

Gives a Sense of the Company's Reputation and Internal Politics

I've seen how power struggles and hidden agendas ruin the workforce. Situations where decision-making processes aren't clear and employees are left in the dark, or how managers align with one executive while the rest support a different perspective are easily alleviated with transparent discussions. As a leader, it is my responsibility to eliminate ambiguity among employees and misconceptions of internal dynamics in the workplace. Open communication enables me to better navigate these dynamics and gives me knowledge of what to do about them.

Boosts Productivity

Imagine a workplace where everyone has uncertain responsi-bilities. They will spend their time deciphering unclear messages and ambiguous information, resulting in an unpleasant work experience and disappointing work perfor-mance. In a transparent workplace, employees will have clear expectations and spend less time trying to understand vague information. Open communication will result in more effective workflows and streamlined processes, leading to higher levels of productivity.

HOW TO CULTIVATE AN HONEST WORK ENVIRONMENT

It Starts With You

You can't always control your team's level of trust, but building accountability is still important. If employees know they can trust you, then you have established a solid foundation. Always be honest and transparent with everything; tell the truth, not just what others want to hear. Even though it might be difficult at times, I'm sure people will always value a leader's honesty. This sends a clear message that transparency is a core value in the organization.

Be Consistent

Building a skyscraper takes time, and so does building trust. Trust is built through consistent honesty. Show that your honesty is not a one-time initiative but a core aspect of your leadership style and company culture.

Exemplify the Behaviors You Want to See in Your Team

Leadership is all about actions, and you must be willing to demonstrate the behaviors that you expect from your team. If you value open communication, actively seek and give feedback; soon, your employees will follow. If transparency is a priority, share information about the company's challenges and decisions. If you made a mistake, acknowledge it. Be a role model and let others see you as an example to follow.

Empower Your Team

Cheerleaders exist for a reason: empowerment. In the workplace, empowerment is more powerful than you might think, especially from a leader. Don't forget to thank your team, celebrate successes together, and elevate their spirits.

Encourage Fun Activities and Socialization

Building solid relationships doesn't always happen through business discussions. Socializing is key, and sometimes we need fun activities to get through our busy days. Encourage employees to be comfortable with each other by supporting laid-back activities, such as board game nights, going out for lunch, or any other relaxing activities. When employees feel connected with each other, they are more likely to communicate freely with their colleagues and superiors.

Provide Avenues for Communication

Establish clear communication channels within the organization, whether it's through online group chats, regular team meetings, or utilizing digital platforms to share ideas. When these avenues are provided, employees will know where to express their ideas.

DIRECT COMMUNICATION TECHNIQUES

What Is It and Why Is It Important?

Direct communication is an exchange of information without any barriers. It involves clear and straightforward communication, where the message is conveyed directly from the sender to the receiver without any distorted meanings.

I remember a childhood game in which a group of players needed to form a line and whisper a message from one person to the next until it reached the last person. If the last person could reiterate the message accurately, the team won. This is what you want to achieve in the organization: coordination and clear messages. Of course, you won't need to deliver the message from one person to the other until it reaches everyone, but if the message you're attempting to deliver is clear, everyone should understand it, and they can pass it to the other people without misinterpretation.

A clear understanding between employees will boost their trust in the workplace. Moreover, it also better prepares everyone for conflicts. If employees are accustomed to communicating problems to each other, they know how to deal with issues faster.

Convey Information Straightforwardly

Take a look at this example: "Hey team, we need to get the project done soon. The deadline is getting near."

This is an example of ambiguous information. I'm sure the team already knows there is a project and a deadline, but what exactly do they need to do? When exactly is "soon?" If you want your messages to be understood, be concise and to the point. Avoid irrelevant information and complicated wording that could confuse the message. Make sure to clearly state the essential points and that the key information is easily identified. Instead of the example above, try something like:

> Our project is due on Friday at 5 p.m. The client is expecting the first draft to be reviewed by next week. Please focus on your assigned tasks and report your progress to me by noon. Communicate any difficulties with me.

The second example provides the necessary details and clear expectations. This method helps employees to swiftly grasp the message.

Marked by Active Listening and Effective Feedback

Don't forget to implement the points from the previous chapter: active listening and effective feedback. Combine these skills with direct communication techniques. Always concentrate on, understand, and respond to your employees' messages. In turn, you will have an easier time when addressing specific problems.

Ensure the Least Amount of Misinterpretation

To convey your message, use concrete and precise phrases. Encourage feedback to ensure that the information was accurately comprehended and be willing to clarify any areas that may have caused confusion. This proactive strategy helps to avoid misunderstandings and keeps everyone on the same page.

NAVIGATING DIFFICULT CONVERSATIONS WITH GEN Z EMPLOYEES

In one case, my team had a conflict with a Gen Z employee at work. We were working on a socialization poster for new recruits. The younger employee suggested using modern, minimalistic, and vibrant elements to appeal to a younger audience, while the senior, more experienced designer suggested classic, neutral, and traditional designs in order to appeal to a wider audience. Both continued to defend their points of view, resulting in unproductive work development.

These cases aren't rare, and they mostly happen because of age gaps. In this situation, it's also challenging to find common ground, especially if both employees don't know how to mediate the problem. In this section, I want to guide you on how to navigate difficult conversations with Gen Z employees. They are not defiant or disobedient; their tendency is to challenge traditional workplace practices, and you must be prepared for many changes.

Understand Their Values and Motivations

Let's take the case I mentioned above. Notice how both employees have different motivations to create the designs. A Gen Z employee preferred minimalistic designs to appeal more to a younger audience, and this is a valid reason. When having a conflict with Gen Z in the workplace, try to understand the motivations behind their actions—they must have something that they need to speak about, and they only need someone to listen.

Use the Right Communication Medium

Gen Z is known for its digital fluency. When addressing a difficult issue, choose the appropriate medium, whether it's a face-to-face conversation, a video call, or a well-crafted message. If I can handle the issue on the spot, I'd rather deal with the problem head-on. However, if the conflict gets intense, I think it's better to let everyone calm down before trying to mediate.

Adopt a Multifaceted Communication Approach

Difficult conversations often benefit from a varied approach. To guarantee that the message is communicated completely, combine verbal communication with visual aids or written documentation. Use examples and scenarios to demonstrate ideas and provide context, allowing Gen Z employees to better understand what is being discussed. In my example provided previously, showing the Gen Z employees some classic poster designs might give them the idea to combine different styles, making teamwork between designers more enjoyable.

Be Open and Transparent

Avoid sugarcoating the problem. You have to communicate the issues and what each employee has to contribute in order to resolve the conflict. For example, if we were to focus solely on minimalistic designs, as the Gen Zer suggested, the company's brand, as it is already known, could be affected. As a result, a senior employee must also contribute to demonstrate how classic designs have always functioned.

SUMMARY

In this chapter, we have explored leadership actions to effectively engage with Gen Z employees in the workplace. Remember, it all starts with you, the leader, to set an example of how others should follow. By being transparent, open, and honest in the workplace, you will gain the trust of Gen Z employees. Your leadership acts as a guiding force in the workplace, impacting workplace dynamics and contributing to the engagement, growth, and success of both Gen Z workers and the company as a whole.

In the next chapter, we will learn how to alleviate Gen Z fears in the workplace and increase their comfort zones.

Chapter Six

UNDERSTANDING AND HELPING TO ALLEVIATE GEN Z FEARS IN THE WORKPLACE

When I was younger and got my first job, I wasn't trained enough to do public speaking. Although I could handle certain aspects of presentations, I struggled with anxiety and a lack of confidence. This affected my work performance since I tended to postpone presentations or let my co-workers take the wheel. This fear of presenting myself in public was one of many problems I had in the workplace, and facing these fears was crucial if I wanted to improve. I couldn't stay in the dark for long, dreading every time it was my turn to present. I asked for feedback, both from my superiors and co-workers, and they gave me one common piece of advice: face it and be yourself.

Though not the most constructive advice, it highlighted my drive to improve. The first step to overcoming fears—and not just in the workplace—is to face them. It takes courage to confront the things that make us uncomfortable, but I acknowledged my fears and tried to confront them, thus opening myself for personal development. Whether it's public speaking, taking on new challenges, or addressing deep-rooted insecurities, facing our fears head-on allows us to break free from their grip and discover our true potential. It may not be easy, but the rewards of conquering our fears are real. Improving my public speaking skills has greatly contributed to my current role as a team manager.

I struggled with my fears when I was a young employee, and I'm sure many Gen Z workers have their own fears in the workplace. To ensure employee growth, it is important to not only focus on their self-awareness but also provide support and encouragement from their leaders. In this chapter, I want to guide you on how to understand and help Gen Z employees face their fears in the workplace while increasing their comfort zones too.

ADDRESSING GEN Z'S WORKPLACE FEARS

Gen Zs are facing a wild and unprecedented future. The workforce for younger generations might be significantly different than they had predicted, and they have to constantly adapt to the development of technology. Let's explore a few common workplace fears a Gen Z might face.

Gen Z's Common Workplace Fears

Lack of Job Opportunities and Experience

I've seen many young people getting concerned about the amount of job opportunities they can get. They constantly see their experiences and knowledge as inadequate because many job requirements are deemed ridiculously demanding.

This is one of the many prominent fears of Gen Zs in the workplace. The concern I have is how companies keep trying to place Gen Zs in the same box as older generations—they're the same only much better at computers. Employers presume Gen Zs have significant knowledge of technology since they are digital natives. While I'm sure many Gen Zs are familiar with electronic gadgets, most businesses have unrealistic expectations. As a result, Gen Zs consider their career options to be limited as they don't have as much experience as older generations do.

Financial Insecurity

Most Gen Zs that are entering the workforce now are still relatively young, and I know a bunch of them are still enrolling in university or pursuing other kinds of education. Student loans aren't cheap, and financial insecurity is bound to be a problem for these youths. Moreover, living costs are constantly increasing, and they are often separated from their families to live alone and make money on their own.

Workplace Stress and Anxiety

Most Gen Zs I know in the workplace have experienced bitter events at their most crucial ages. Between age 18 to their early 20s, they had to graduate online and focus their connections through online meetings due to the COVID-19 pandemic, which heavily impacted their stress and anxiety. During this age, people are mostly exploring their lives and stepping into the workforce with excitement. Everyone is familiar with the feelings of stress and anxiety, but many Gen Zers must come to terms with the reality of embarking on their careers with uncertain expectations. Not knowing what your future looks like is an incredible weight to shoulder, and these fears continue in the workplace.

Mental Health Challenges

The workforce is getting busier. Companies are eager to accept new recruits, and they expect big successes. One of the many things I'm concerned about is the emotional well-being of my employees, especially the younger ones. As Gen Z deals with economic downturns, difficulties in getting a job, and many global problems, mental health becomes more worrying. Luckily, they are more aware of mental health challenges. However, there are still workplace cultures that aren't prioritizing their employee's mental health, and this could be a major fear for Gen Z employees.

Navigating Workplace Culture

As we are aware, most Gen Z employees are still young. They have a lot of challenges when it comes to adapting to the workforce, especially if it's their first time entering a job. Once, they had to deal with how schools operated with online classes and meetings through video conferences. Now, the abrupt changes from WFO (Work From Office) culture to remote and hybrid work can be overwhelming. The rapidly changing methods of work are bound to give Gen Z employees fears in the workplace.

How Can These Challenges Be Alleviated?

Besides all the methods I've laid out in the previous chapters, there are more practical methods for you to alleviate Gen Z fears in the workplace and help them increase their comfort zones.

Soft Skills Training

According to a survey, 46% of Gen Z workers ask their employers to prioritize soft skills training in the workplace (Wicklethewait, 2023). Why is this important? Remote or hybrid work has hindered spontaneous office interactions for many Gen Z workers, impacting their essential communication skills. When young employees don't know how to be proactive in their communication, they will have difficulties in sharing their thoughts and collaborating with the team.

One way to help your younger employees speak up is to synergize with them. Instead of making them the center of attention while presenting or speaking, guide the Gen Z employee through brainstorming or quick polls with other team members. When Gen Zs see their audience engaged and having fun, they will have more confidence.

Mindfulness Meditation

Mindfulness is a practice that involves bringing one's attention to the present moment in a non-judgmental and accepting way. It is about being fully aware of our thoughts, feelings, bodily sensations, and the surrounding environment. Mindfulness can be cultivated through various techniques such as meditation, breathing exercises, and conscious awareness of daily activities. It has been shown to reduce stress, improve focus and concentration, enhance emotional well-being, and promote mental health.

There are a lot of mindfulness meditation books and guides out there, and I recommend you give those resources to your Gen Z employees. Encourage them to focus on the task at hand and be mindful of their actions. The methods are simple, but they need some time to practice. Incorporating mindfulness in the workplace will alleviate their stressors and help them deal with everyday challenges.

Work-Life Balance

Gen Zs are attached to their personal lives, and they don't want a career that takes away their individual freedom. They want to have a career that supports their personal development, not just provide them with a salary. That's why work-life balance is important for them. They are more likely to request days off than your older employees, and you might need to accommodate them.

Mental Health Support

Make sure your company is accommodating mental health support for employees. Gen Zs are normalizing the importance of mental health support, which can enhance employee work performance.

Physical and Spiritual Wellbeing

The increase in digital well-being tools, such as workout routine apps, calorie trackers, and other mobile apps, is increasing Gen Z's awareness of their well-being. A survey by UNiDAYS in 2018 suggested that around 43% of Gen Zs like to work out at home and 65% of them use fitness apps. This is a nice development for their health, and you can encourage Gen Zs to exercise daily to promote a healthy work environment, using team reminders, awareness posters, or allowing workouts during office hours.

Career Progression

Unclear progression is one of the biggest problems for Gen Z youths. In education systems, schools usually provide a mentor to guide students on how to progress in their education—whether to continue to university or acquire a certain skill certificate to jump into the workforce. To make sure that Gen Z employees have a vision for their future careers, you can try implementing the same counseling system.

Community and Connection

Creating a sense of connection in the workplace is crucial for Gen Z. They like to have meaningful connections, especially if the people around them have common interests and values. Encourage team-building activities to foster an emotional connection between Gen Z and older generations in the workplace.

Building Confidence and Resilience

Enhanced Onboarding

An onboarding program is a planned procedure that helps new workers become acquainted with their jobs, responsibilities, and the organization they are joining. It usually consists of orientation meetings, training, introductions to important team members, and giving necessary resources to help new employees integrate smoothly into the organization. An onboarding program's purpose is to make new workers feel welcomed, supported, and prepared to thrive in their new position. Implementing an onboarding program can provide useful information about the company's culture, expectations, and opportunities for growth, which boosts Gen Z's confidence at work.

Flexible scheduling

Before Gen Z entered the workforce, the only work routine I knew was to go to a physical office where we had to commute to work every day, from morning to evening. Then, the pandemic occurred, and Gen Zs started working in hybrid and remote setups. This, in turn, resulted in older workers having to adapt to the changing situations. Gen Z individuals prefer flexible work schedules to accommodate their fast-paced lifestyles and educational pursuits.

Social Responsibility

As we know, Gen Zs tend to prioritize a sustainable lifestyle. They want to make sure that the company they are working for is engaging in ethical practices. Knowing this priority, you can try implementing social responsibility in the workplace. This helps to build their confidence in their work, knowing that they engage in social topics.

Corporate Social Responsibility (CSR) refers to a company's commitment to operating in an ethical and sustainable manner, while also considering the impact of its actions on society and the environment. It involves taking responsibility for the company's impact on various stakeholders, including employees, customers, communities, and the environment. CSR initiatives can include philanthropy, environmental sustainability efforts, ethical business practices, employee volunteering programs, and more. The goal of CSR is to go beyond profit-making and contribute positively to society.

DIGITAL OR IN-PERSON COMMUNICATION?

Gen Z Is Comfortable and Adept at Digital Communication

When working with Gen Z, you can rely on them being able to utilize digital tools with ease. From smartphones to social media platforms, they are adept at navigating the digital landscape. Their fluency in technology allows them to quickly adapt to new software, apps, and online platforms, making them valuable assets in today's digital-driven workforce. Whether it's collaborating on virtual projects, conducting research online, or leveraging social media for marketing purposes, Gen Z's digital proficiency opens up a world of possibilities for seamless and efficient communication and productivity.

Most Responsive to Visual Communication

We've learned the importance of visual communication to engage Gen Zs in the workplace. They are proficient at visual interactions, and you can use this to your advantage. Visual communication tends to be more concise and clear, and Gen Zs know how to respond. As a result, Gen Zs have developed a keen understanding of visual cues and are adept at interpreting and responding to visual communication.

They Value In-Person Communication Too

Despite their digital fluency, Gen Z knows the importance of face-to-face interactions. Experts were surprised when they found out how many Gen Z individuals value more direct interactions with people as opposed to our basic understanding of Gen Zs being more digitally connected. Due to their extensive online interactions, Gen Zs crave meaningful face-to-face communication and cannot solely rely on constant screen time.

RECOMMENDATIONS FOR MANAGERS

Balance Digital and In-Person Communication

Digital communication isn't always effective. Sometimes, people need to see instructions in front of their eyes to understand the message. There will also be some instances where employees might have difficulties navigating an unfamiliar digital tool. If you only rely on electronic messages, information tends to get jumbled up and confusing, not to mention the possibility of information overload. When technology isn't doing the trick, it's time for face-to-face interactions.

Get to Know Their Communication Styles

It is critical to understand individual preferences among the Gen Z cohort. Some people thrive on digital communication, while others prefer face-to-face interactions. As their manager, you should take the time to learn your team members' communication styles and customize your approaches accordingly.

SUMMARY

Let's recall back to the main point of this chapter: the best way to eliminate fear is to face it head-on. In order to face our fears, we first need to acknowledge them. You have learned the unique struggles Gen Z workers are experiencing right now, and it's time for you, as the leader, to create a comfortable work environment for Gen Z. Be supportive, encouraging, understanding, and respectful of their worker demands.

Gen Z's struggles are distinct, encompassing an uncertain future, financial instability, and the challenges of an evolving workforce. In the upcoming chapter, we will explore how these unique challenges contribute to their individual identities, and it is important to recognize the diverse individualities within the Gen Z cohort to create an inclusive workplace.

Chapter Seven

ACKNOWLEDGING INDIVIDUALITY ACROSS THE GEN Z COHORT

Not all Zoomers zoom the same way, and it's important to discover the unique speeds and styles of your Gen Z team. Gen Z, like previous generations, brings a myriad of talents, experiences, and communication preferences to the table. Other than that, cultural, religious, and other social upbringings can be huge factors in shaping their personalities.

Have you ever wondered why there are various "aesthetic" styles of younger people in popular media? While these styles are not new in general, Gen Zs are embracing these lifestyles once again. This includes their fashion choices, the media they consume (movies, music, or TV shows), hobbies, and more. This creates a sense of community, a collection of people of similar tastes, and as a result, they are making these lifestyles part of their core personalities. For example, I know a Gen Z employee who dresses in an oldies style—wears a vintage watch, has a leather suitcase, and brings antique pens. The same applies to other styles, like sporting vibrant clothing reminiscent of an 80s teenager and enjoying sitcoms during their leisure time. Some of them seem to be unfazed by the development of trends because they recognize these styles as who they are.

In the workplace, I thought working with Gen Z employees would make technical work easier since they've adapted to digital tools, but some of them have varied preferences when using technology. Even the smallest debate such as using Android or Apple devices can create disagreements.

These differences are just a few examples, and you are going to face even more out there. As leaders, embracing these differences is one of our main duties and can result in more cohesive and beneficial team chemistry.

In this chapter, I want to guide you on recognizing and addressing Gen Z's individual needs and styles within their own cohort. This will help to personalize their work and communication strategies.

RECOGNIZING, ASSESSING, AND RESPONDING TO INDIVIDUAL NEEDS OF EMPLOYEES

You can't expect every Gen Z individual to have the exact same needs. Even though most of them may share core values, there will still be differences. Someone who grew up in a low-income family may have different priorities than someone who grew up with financial stability. This is where you need to be sensitive to each Gen Z employee's needs.

Recognize Individual Needs

Recognizing the various aspirations that each Gen Z employee has is not an easy feat. Some of them may need to build long-lasting connections and aim to progress their career to the next level; some of them might need to learn new fields of expertise to broaden their knowledge. The easiest process in recognizing these needs is what people like to call the Maslow Hierarchy of Needs, a psychology theory developed in 1943 by Abraham Maslow.

Think of needs as a pyramid: the base needs to be strong in order to build a solid structure. The base of these needs is physiological, such as sleeping, eating, and so on. The second structure consists of safety and security in life. The third and fourth structures begin to involve psychological needs: social, relationships, and self-accomplishments. Lastly, the fifth structure is self-fulfillment and the strong potential to continue striving for the best of self.

Notice how the top of the pyramid focuses on the capacity to continue to the next level. When Gen Zs join your organization, they will have wants and needs, and I guarantee that they wish for a higher purpose. So, focus on their individual goals and recognize what they want to achieve in the future.

Assess Employee Skills and Performance

Let's consider a scenario: a Gen Z employee, Maya, entered my company as a web designer, and after four months, it was time for her performance assessment. As the manager, I like to begin by recognizing their individual aspirations. Maya expressed a strong interest in working on collaborative projects, meaning that she prefers to interact with the team and make the work environment enjoyable for everyone. I acknowledged this and noted her excellent communication skills, particularly towards the team.

Now it's time to assess her skills and performance in the workplace. In this step, I like to use a business framework called KPI (Key Performance Indicator). KPIs are goals that align with the individual and the organization. I will start by assessing Maya's individual contributions to the team and how her skills have improved since the first week of joining. In this stage, I would involve other team members to give her constructive feedback on what she needs to improve.

After assessing her performance, I acknowledge her successes and offer more guidance for future progressions. This thorough assessment will have a positive impact for the employee in the long run.

Respond to Employee Needs

To continue the above example, one day, Maya messaged me about needing to learn more design skills to gain more experience in media marketing. After discussing this goal, I realized that Maya excelled with a hands-on approach to learning, so I arranged a mentorship for her with a senior team member.

Responding to Gen Z's needs is necessary for the company's success because ensuring that an employee's needs are fulfilled increases their likelihood of being loyal to the company.

Promote Employee Satisfaction

After the three steps above are done, I continue to build a healthy work-life balance for Gen Z employees, initiating regular check-ins to ensure that their needs are addressed. I also explore flexible work schedules to allow time for self-paced online courses and self-learning. This will enhance the overall job satisfaction among the Gen Z team.

HOW TO IDENTIFY INDIVIDUAL COMMUNICATION STYLES

A communication style has various aspects of expressing oneself to other people, such as verbal and non-verbal communication, tone of voice, body language, and choice of words. Communication styles can vary from person to person and can be influenced by both external and internal factors.

The workplace today consists of multiple generations working together. Understanding Gen Z's communication styles can be challenging because they bring newer means of communication. Here are a few ways for you to identify individual communication styles across the Gen Z cohort and determine which ones would be the best to interact with them professionally.

Through Observation and Interaction

The first thing I like to do is observe how they conduct themselves formally and informally. This will require team members and supervisors to actively engage with Gen Z employees and figure out how they interact with each other on a daily basis. Face-to-face conversations, online discussions, and meetings can be a great way to figure out their communication patterns.

By Asking Direct Questions

There's nothing more straightforward than asking their preferred means of communication directly. I like them to share their comfort levels with different methods of communication, whether it's through email, phone calls, video meetings, or instant messaging.

By Using Assessment Tools

Assessment tools are helpful in analyzing and categorizing different communication styles. Here are a couple assessment tools you can use:

- Neuro-linguistic Communication Profile (NCP)

Communication is not always about auditory cues. In fact, it extends far beyond spoken words. Non-verbal communication, such as body language, facial expressions, and gestures, plays a significant role in conveying messages. These non-verbal cues often speak louder than words, so you need to understand the complex nuances of communication.

NCP is a field that explores the relationships between thought processes, language, and behavioral patterns. This method has been used to assess workplace communication, personal development, and psychotherapy. This assessment tool includes 60 questions related to communication styles, and a profile will be made based on these characteristics. Participants will be able to review their strengths and weaknesses and what they need to do to become effective communicators.

- Team Communication Inventory

This assessment tool is commonly used as a survey, designed to evaluate various aspects of team communication. This tool helps to identify strengths, weaknesses, and areas that need improvement in team communication.

The components of this tool include assessing communication preferences, team members' listening skills, clarity in communicating, feedback mechanisms, conflict resolutions, and others.

By Understanding Communication Style Frameworks

There are many communication style frameworks, but there are two that are mainly useful in the workplace.

DiSC Assessment Framework

The DiSC personality framework is a widely used behavioral assessment tool that categorizes individuals into four main personality types: dominance (D), influence (I), steadiness (S), and conscientiousness (C). It helps individuals gain insights into their own behavioral tendencies and understand how they interact with others in various situations.

The DiSC model, invented by psychologist William Moulton Marston in the 1920s, was later improved and popularized by Walter Vernon Clarke in the 1950s. Today, many organizations use the DiSC evaluation to improve communication, team dynamics, leadership development, and interpersonal connections in the workplace.

Here is a brief overview of the different categories:

- dominant

The keywords for this personality type are decisive, efficient, intense, result-oriented, competitive, and risk-tolerant. People who possess this personal style are also known as the "director" or the "driver" of situations. They love to be in control, get down to business, and be blunt. Sometimes they might have tunnel vision, but a goal-focused person will be important in your team.

- influence

The keywords for this personality type are outgoing, enthusiastic, persuasive, relationship-oriented, lively, and optimistic. They are the "initiator" in your team, thriving in interpersonal relationships and teamwork. When interacting with the influencers, it's best to be casual and let your uniqueness show. These people are valuable assets in your team as they will be the ones who tie everyone together.

- steady

The keywords for this personality type are cooperative, relaxed, patient, supportive, friendly, and thorough. They are the "steadfast" members of the team, making sure everyone is cooperating and in harmony. They value consistency, stability, and loyalty. Most of them adapt quickly and often take service roles such as at a help desk or customer service. You can't build a skyscraper without a strong base, and steady people are what you need to ensure your team stays strong in unity.

- conscientious

The keywords for this personality type are systematic, logical, reserved, process-oriented, cautious, and risk-averse. They are the "careful" people in your team, prioritizing responsibility, honesty, and precision. They rely on logical thinking and are usually the ones who are suitable for analytic roles. Conscientious people are highly systematic, and they are valuable when running risk assessments.

Analytical, Functional, Intuitive, and Personal

These categories are identified by author Mark Murphy to define your communication style. Here is a brief overview of each category:

- analytical

Numbers, data, and facts—these are the main fuels for analytical communicators. They are dependable when it comes to making ideas come true with facts and figures. They want others to be straightforward, blunt, and be in the present moment. When interacting with analytical communicators, it's best to offer a clear project outline and state your expectations.

- functional

Functional communicators are organized people. Some people meticulously plan every aspect of their tasks, including when, where, what they need, and how they will execute their plans. Some people might see them as uptight and inflexible, but they can be relied upon to get everything done. For functional communicators, it's suggested that you give clear timelines for projects and expect them to ask many questions as they will always seek clarity.

- intuitive

Have you ever wondered why some people might be overly optimistic? Intuitive communicators often have this mindset as they are the big thinkers in your team. Once they have a strong purpose, they will pursue it however they can, often already having strong visualizations of their success. Intuitive communicators are great at staying motivated and redirecting your team back to a common goal. When working with intuitive communicators, trust them to be creative—they rely on intuition after all. Give them room to brainstorm and generate ideas.

- personal

Some people understand others better than they understand themselves. Personal communicators are highly sensitive to people's feelings, they always focus on interpersonal awareness, and they rely on diplomacy. They want to make sure everyone is in harmony, which in turn will boost emotional relationships in the team. They might care more about others' well-being than the goal, which is also a part of how that goal might be achieved. Personal communicators want to be heard as much as they want to hear you. Give them opportunities to be emotional and allow them to connect with team members.

HOW GEN ZS ASSERT THEIR INDIVIDUALITY IN THE WORKPLACE

Individuality is not all about selfishness. It encompasses the unique qualities, perspectives, and contributions that each person brings to the table. It celebrates diversity and encourages self-expression, allowing individuals to shine in their own authentic way. Embracing individuality fosters a sense of empowerment as it recognizes that each person has their own strengths and talents to offer. It is through embracing and respecting individuality that we can create a more inclusive and vibrant society.

Embracing Self-Expression

If you've scrolled social media long enough, you'll find that most younger people are vibrant in expressing themselves online, whether it's as simple as walking their dog outside, sharing their vacation pictures, or posting photos of their lunch. Some people might see this as attention-seeking, but we've never had a closer form of self-appreciation than this. For the most part, sharing a portion of your life doesn't necessarily mean you're trying to get attention, but it's a way to express gratitude. Sharing news of your career promotion with your family doesn't make you self-absorbed or selfish. It's simply a way to share a happy moment in your life and celebrate with your loved ones.

I've seen a lot of Gen Z employees are more comfortable and open with their self-expression, and I think that's a good thing. Accept the individuality of your Gen Z employees and let their uniqueness shine in their work.

Demanding Flexibility and Work-Life Balance

Gen Zs are still young in the workplace, meaning they need more time to adjust their work schedules and must be careful not to burn out too quickly. Moreover, they are aware of the consequences of overworking as a result of being more aware of emotional well-being. We all know unbalanced working hours will have negative effects on the overall working system. Tired and burned-out employees are no good to have in the workplace, and Gen Zs are fighting for this work flexibility.

Seeking Meaning and Purpose

Believe it or not, most Gen Z motivations in the workplace aren't all about the big pay. A survey from Visier found that around 75% of the US Gen Z population aged 18 to 24 want a career to have self-fulfillment, as this is more important than the salary (Nawrat, 2022). If they have a clear purpose, they will carry out this passion and learn more things to achieve income.

Valuing Transparency

Social media is full of filters and double personas, and learning how to be transparent with other people is a Gen Z interest. They expect other people to be transparent too, and they desire an environment where everyone is honest and respectful towards each other, without any barriers.

Seeking Opportunities for Growth and Learning

Gen Zs have a lot to learn, and they want to do things that let them grow and learn to adapt to the future of the workforce. I still see many businesses are reluctant to give younger employees the training for they need, simply because companies automatically assume they are already good at everything. People need to learn in order to improve, and a leader must facilitate these learning opportunities to create a brighter future for employees.

Aligning With Companies That Share Their Values

In the same survey by Visier, it was revealed that 82% of Gen Z workers want to work for ethical employers (Nawrat, 2022). They want their values to be seen. They seek out organizations that prioritize inclusivity by fostering a sense of belonging for individuals from all backgrounds. Moreover, Gen Zs are drawn to companies that demonstrate a strong commitment to social and environmental responsibility. They are more likely to support businesses that actively contribute to positive change and sustainability efforts. By aligning themselves with inclusive and responsible companies, Gen Zs feel empowered to make a difference and contribute to a better future.

SUMMARY

When discussing the individuality of Gen Z, it can be said that their most defining characteristic is their refusal to be confined to a single category. Not all of them are obsessed with fame and fortune, and not all of them prioritize the same things. The individuality of Gen Z is the fact that they want to be different, and they are brave to show this. To create an inclusive workplace, you must know how to acknowledge these differences.

This topic ties us to the next chapter: in accepting Gen Z's individual differences, we create a path for them to show their innovation and creativity.

Part Four

MOBILIZE INNOVATION AND ADAPT TO CHANGE

Chapter Eight

FOSTERING INNOVATION AND CREATIVITY

I nnovation is the currency of the future, and Gen Z is rich with it. With their fresh perspectives and innate ability to think outside the box, Gen Z is poised to revolutionize the way we live, work, and interact. From developing ground-breaking apps to spearheading social movements, Gen Z is at the forefront of shaping the future. Their entrepreneurial spirit and passion for making a difference are driving them to challenge traditional norms. As the torchbearers of progress, Gen Z is not only rich with ideas but also determined to turn them into reality, propelling society forward into a new era of possibilities.

Gen Z is known to be the generation of innovators. There have been a number of Gen Z individuals who contributed greatly to the development of technology and its future. One notable inventor is Palmer Luckey, the creator of Oculus VR. Oculus is a device that allows users to experience a simulated reality in a headset. It offers extensive visual tracking capabilities, providing a sense of realism that makes video games and movies feel like real-life experiences. It's a ground-breaking innovation that revolutionized the world of multimedia industry, and its innovation is still in progress. Luckey was just 19 years old when he created the Oculus headset in his parents' basement ("3 Identities," 2023).

Another inventor is Easton LaChappelle, who managed to build a robotic arm made from LEGOs. At the age of 17, his inventions led him to create a 3D-printed robotic arm ("3 Identities," 2023). LaChappelle is now the founder of Unlimited Tomorrow, a company that creates prosthetic limbs using 3D printing technology.

These are only a couple of examples of young innovators. If all Gen Zs are being taught to live up to their full potential, imagine what many other innovations they can make to shape our future. In this chapter, I want to guide you on how to create a space that supports Gen Z's potential, fostering a workplace that embraces innovation and creativity.

GEN Z'S CHALLENGES IN WORKPLACE CREATIVITY AND INNOVATION

Gen Zs have a lot of technological advantages. However, this generation isn't without its challenges when it comes to embracing their own abilities to create and innovate. Besides their drive to pursue newer things, Gen Z knows a lot about how money works, and they're interested in being financially independent. Businesses provide a perfect opportunity for them to earn money and gain a lot of experience. According to a survey by Samsung ("Gen Z," 2023), around 50% of Gen Zers are interested in starting their own business. This shows that they have an entrepreneurial mindset, yet there are still obstacles preventing them from unleashing their full potential. What are they?

Managing Complexity and Ambiguity

Gen Z's characteristics are complex. I found many leaders, and Gen Zs themselves, were immersed in a work environment with unprecedented complexity and ambiguity. Gen Z employees need time to define their identities, yet technological advancements, global interconnectivity, and the changing nature of industries pose challenges that demand adaptability and critical thinking. Unlike the more structured environments of the past, Gen Zs need to navigate unknown territories and make new solutions to more complex problems. Adapting to this complexity can be overwhelming, impacting their ability to unleash their creativity.

Lack of Soft Skills Training

While Gen Zs excel in technical skills, there is a noticeable gap when it comes to interpersonal skills and emotional control. We know that Gen Zs are on a path to challenge traditional means of education, but unfortunately, most of them grew up in the traditional system, which often falls short in developing these skills. As a result, Gen Zs may struggle to build professional relationships with their older colleagues and effectively communicate their ideas. The absence of comprehensive soft skills training hinders their capacity to be innovative in the workplace.

Communication Differences

Gen Zs embrace instant messaging, emojis, and shorter content, which can clash with the communication styles of older employees and superiors. These differences are prone to create misunderstandings.

HOW TO UNLOCK GEN Z'S CREATIVE POTENTIAL

Encourage Them to Generate Ideas

There's a popular internet saying that goes, "If it is stupid but it works, it isn't stupid." Do you agree? Ideas can be half-baked, seemingly bad, or intangible; however, these ideas are the main driving point to generate even more ideas. I'm sure Easton LaChappelle didn't stop making his LEGO robot arm when people told him it was a ridiculous idea. If you want your Gen Z employees to be creative and innovative, encourage their ideas, even if it may seem strange at first. Allow them to take their time and refine their ideas—they might discover something unimaginable.

Brainstorming and Mind Mapping

Whenever a Gen Zer proposes a new idea, I always encourage them to have brainstorming sessions to stimulate creative thinking. Mind mapping is also a good technique to provide a structured yet flexible approach to problem-solving. I absolutely love mind mapping as it allows Gen Z employees to explore various perspectives and generate solutions collaboratively.

Promote Freedom and Flexibility

You can't rush a genius. The best creative worker is the one who's given enough time to flesh out their ideas, allowing them to experiment in different ways. Flexibility not only enhances their sense of ownership in their own ideas but also nurtures an atmosphere where out-of-the-box thinking is welcomed.

Build a Diverse Team

A team with a mix of skills, expertise, backgrounds, and perspectives will be the catalyst of innovation, and Gen Zs thrive in an inclusive environment. Each team member brings their unique set of experiences and knowledge to the table, allowing for a broader range of ideas and solutions to be explored. The combination of different skill sets ensures that all aspects of a project or problem are thoroughly examined, leading to more creative and effective outcomes. Moreover, diverse perspectives foster a culture of inclusivity and open-mindedness, encouraging collaboration and the exchange of ideas.

Work on Individual Strengths

There is a popular saying that if you teach a fish to climb a tree, the fish will forever think it is stupid—it simply can't happen because fish are meant to thrive in water. This is also how you should see your Gen Z employees. Get to know which areas they thrive in the most and focus on that instead of trying to teach them something entirely new.

Provide the Right Resources

Equip Gen Z with the necessary resources to fuel their creativity. By providing access to cutting-edge technology, mentorship programs, and creative spaces, we can empower the next generation to unleash their full creative potential. Whether it's through digital tools, art supplies, or educational programs, investing in the resources that foster creativity will not only benefit individuals but also contribute to the overall growth and innovation of our society. Let's create an environment where Gen Z can thrive and express their unique ideas in the workplace, paving the way for a brighter and more imaginative future.

Encourage Risk-Taking

Fortune favors the bold, they said, and this is true in the workplace as well. Taking risks and stepping out of one's comfort zone often leads to great opportunities and success. In a competitive professional environment, I like to encourage Gen Z to take bold actions, make innovative decisions, and embrace challenges to make them stand out and achieve their goals. Whether it's pitching a groundbreaking idea, pursuing a new project, or speaking up in meetings, when Gen Zs are bold in the workplace, they can open doors to advancement and recognition. However, it's important to strike a balance between boldness and careful consideration as reckless actions can have negative consequences. So, remember to educate them on taking calculated risks and how to seize opportunities that come their way in the workplace.

Encourage Daydreaming

Who says daydreaming is only wasting time? Scientific research by Kem et al. (2021) has proven that daydreaming brings many benefits, such as reducing anxiety and stress and helping to clear our minds. A study by McMillan et al. in 2013 also revealed that daydreaming is correlated with higher levels of creativity. Additionally, a study of college students conducted by Baird et al. (2012) showed that daydreaming is linked to a 41% increase in creativity and productivity. So, encourage your Gen Z employees to do a little bit of daydreaming when faced with an obstacle.

Distance From Noise

The ability to focus is different for many people, but generally, a little less noise will be good for our concentration. Silence can create an environment for our brain to focus, allowing us to perform tasks more effectively. When different noises enter our brains at the same time, we become distracted. Silence is also an important part of the creative process. Great scientists like Albert Einstein and Sir Isaac Newton worked in solitude most of their lives because silence allowed them to solely focus on their craft. If you want your Gen Z employees to work more effectively, eliminating distracting noise is a main priority.

Experimental Learning

I always allow Gen Z employees to implement hands-on learning. Experiment with their ideas and teach them not to be ashamed if they make a mistake. Making mistakes is the key to improvement and this can be a big opportunity for them to develop their ideas further.

MEASURE THE SUCCESS OF CREATIVITY AND INNOVATION

Creativity and innovation won't come from pure happenstance, luck, or a blessing; they are the result of deliberate effort, tireless exploration, and a relentless pursuit of new ideas. Some days ideas seem to materialize out of thin air, like a lightbulb above your head. But how can you consistently generate these lightbulb moments? Moreover, how can you motivate team members to keep generating these ideas? How should you reward them? Monitoring these processes is essential to figure out what influences innovation and how to increase it.

Trying to measure creativity is akin to locating the source of life within a body. Dissecting the body into individual parts such as the head, heart, lungs, etc., results in isolated components that do not make "life." Measuring creativity means recognizing that its essence lies not in a singular detail, but in the combination of various aspects. Here are a few ways for you to measure creativity and innovation in your team.

Quantitative Metrics

Number of New Ideas and Processes Launched

Use a quantitative scale to measure the novelty and impact of each idea and process introduced by team members. Then, regularly review the report on the cumulative number of new ideas launched over a specific time period—for example, every four months or every year.

Profit Growth

Identify the revenue generated from new products and innovative business models. Establish clear benchmarks to measure your profit growth and conduct a cost-benefit analysis to identify the return on investment.

Number of Patents Filed

Tracking filed patents provides valuable insights into a company's innovative activities and serves as a quantitative measure of the innovative capacity. The number of filed patents is a tangible metric—a higher number of patent filings generally suggests a greater innovation within the company. You can also use these measures to compare the number of filed patents with peer industries which gives insight into your company's competitive position.

Research and Development Spending

Research and development (R&D) expenses are budgets used to research and develop new products. To measure the innovation of your team, you can correlate R&D spending with the successful launches of new products and assess how efficient R&D investments are by comparing them with the number of innovations introduced.

Percentage of Ideas Implemented From Ideation Sessions

Whenever a team member pitches a fresh idea, track and monitor how many ideas are generated during brainstorming sessions. Then, calculate the percentage of ideas from these sessions that are successfully implemented. To quantify these ideas, you can identify the patterns that prove to be most feasible for implementation.

Qualitative Metrics

Employee Engagement Scores

To shift into qualitative measures, surveys and feedback are great sources to measure your team's innovative development. Employee engagement surveys can capture the subjective experiences of each employee regarding the company's support to develop innovation. Open-ended questions allow employees to share their personal insights and suggestions in contributing to a richer creative dynamic in the workplace.

Customer Satisfaction With New Offerings

Keeping track of qualitative feedback from customers who have experienced new products or services can provide valuable insight into innovation development. Additionally, you can conduct customer interviews and focus groups, or ask for written testimonials to reveal how innovative offerings can meet customer expectations.

Expert Evaluations of Innovation Quality

Involving external experts or industry specialists to evaluate the quality of your team's innovation can be a valuable resource as they will add an objective layer to qualitative assessments. Experts can offer insights based on their experience and compare creative outputs with other industry standards.

Leadership Perception of Innovation Culture

An innovative team comes from a supportive leader. You can conduct qualitative interviews or surveys with other team leaders and uncover their perceptions of the innovation culture in the workplace. Leaders can share knowledge and express attitudes, support, and commitment to create an innovative culture. This provides a deeper understanding of a leader's importance in driving innovation.

Process and Behavioral Metrics

Cross-Functional Collaboration on Innovation Projects

To measure innovative development in the workplace, you can evaluate the degree of cross-collaboration within projects by tracking the team's involvement with different departments. Then, qualitatively assess the communication's efficacy and mutual support demonstrated by team members from diverse expertise areas.

Employee Participation Rates in Ideation Programs

Track the number of active employees participating in brainstorming sessions then assess the quality of participation by considering factors such as different ideas presented, engagement levels, and enthusiasm during sessions.

Cycle Time of Innovation Process

Measure the time taken for an innovative idea to progress then examine the adaptability and responsiveness of team members through the process, including their ability to overcome challenges when necessary.

Willingness to Take Risks and Learning From Mistakes

Develop a metric that tracks instances where team members took calculated risks and adapted quickly, fostering a fail-fast and continuous learning culture. Then, you can qualitatively assess the team's attitude towards risk-taking, embracing failure as a learning opportunity.

Trend Analysis

Track Innovation Metrics Over Time

Monitor the evolution of key process metrics, such as the speed of innovation, the cycle time, and the efficiency of ideation programs. Then, analyze how these metrics have changed over time to identify trends and patterns.

Benchmark Innovation Performance Against Competitors

Compare innovation metrics with industry standards or competitors, such as the number of new ideas implemented, profit growth, and R&D spending. You can also explore qualitative aspects, such as innovation culture through surveys and questionnaires. Benchmarking against industry standards leads to a broader perspective on your team's innovation standing.

SUMMARY

Now you've learned how creative and innovative Gen Zs can be if given the right environment. These bright youths are the future of technology, and they will be even more capable if the workplace they're in is supportive of fresh ideas. The most important thing to create an innovative culture is the willingness to take risks and see mistakes as an opportunity to learn.

Innovation will increase productivity in the workplace as it provides employees with fresh materials to work on. However, Gen Zs are struggling with a new kind of problem: digital overload. How do we balance digital use for productivity and entertainment? We will find out in the next chapter.

Chapter Nine

BALANCING DIGITAL OVERLOAD

F inding balance is the key to productivity in the age of digital overload. During the pandemic, I remember when everything had to be done online, from team meetings to classes and connecting with family members. Digital fatigue is a real thing, even among Gen Z individuals. I've seen them struggle with constant online connections. As humans, we all crave intimate connections, and we cannot solely rely on the virtual world.

As we recover from the aftermath of the pandemic, we begin to see the importance of balance between digital and physical connections. We have started to be aware of how to achieve balance in this digital era as we no longer want to be bound by prolonged online communications.

With the constant influx of information and distractions, Gen Z easily gets overwhelmed and loses focus. However, by implementing effective strategies, one can regain control of our time and energy. By finding the right balance between technology and personal well-being, Gen Zs can optimize productivity and lead a more fulfilling life in this digital age.

In this chapter, I want to guide you on how to manage digital distractions and promote a balanced digital work environment, especially among Gen Z members in the organization.

MANAGING DIGITAL DISTRACTIONS

We all agree that owning a smartphone feels like a priority as we practically can't live without it. It stores our important data, from bank accounts to our social personas. Ever since I owned a smartphone, I constantly find myself distracted by it, and it has visibly affected my productivity. For example, while I'm working on my laptop, a single blip of the screen or notification alert immediately scatters my attention. Suddenly, I find myself scrolling through social media on my phone and watching YouTube videos when I'm supposed to be working.

I don't doubt that most of us have experienced something like this—it only takes a tiny distraction to interrupt your work altogether. A study revealed that Millennials and Gen Z are the most likely workers to describe themselves as digitally distracted while they're working (Udemy Business, 2018.) So, how can we manage these digital distractions and make the most of our working hours?

Strategies for Minimizing Digital Interruptions

Set Clear Boundaries and Policies

It's fundamental to establish clear policies regarding digital device usage in the workplace. Often, employees are easily distracted from their work due to their constant use of electronic devices. In the workplace, I like to implement a rule where employees have to limit phone usage. I let them establish the boundaries themselves and let them work at their own pace. For example, a Gen Z employee prefers to distance themselves from their phone for 30 minutes before going back to work. Additionally, disabling notification alerts and prohibiting the use of social media apps on work devices is also effective. You can communicate these boundaries and make it clear how important it is to minimize digital interruptions in the workplace.

Promote Focus and Mindfulness

There are cases where people get enraged by a single social media post. When this happens, they can completely lose touch with reality and get emotional, throwing tantrums no matter their surroundings. Practicing focus and mindfulness can help with this problem. In the workplace, implement short breaks for employees to help recharge their energy and refocus on the present moment. Providing them with resources and training in time management can also help with their task prioritization.

Nurture Engagement and Connectedness

A workplace where each employee is connected and open to each other is a workplace with minimum distraction. When workers feel connected to their colleagues, they are more likely to focus on their tasks and be less susceptible to digital distractions.

Design Workspaces to Minimize Distractions

Many workplaces now implement workspace designs to minimize distractions, such as quiet zones, noise-canceling tools, and relaxing rooms. These arrangements help employees to work in a conducive environment that boosts their concentration.

Promote Flexibility

Did you know that children of strict parents tend to rebel the most? When people are put into tight schedules with little room to breathe on their own, their fuel to work effectively will run out faster. Burning out will happen more often, therefore they will seek external stimulation, such as using their phone for entertainment.

Flexibility is important for Gen Z employees to minimize distractions in the workplace. When they have the autonomy to manage their schedules and choose how to approach tasks at their own pace, Gen Zs will have a better sense of responsibility to finish their work. This boosts their productivity as well as reduces the temptation to succumb to digital distractions.

Lead by Example

Last but not least, being a leader means you need to be the role model for behaviors you wish to see in your team members. Avoid unnecessary interruptions during meetings or while interacting with your employees. Don't use your phone while in meetings and don't talk to someone else while an employee is trying to talk to you. When leaders lead by example, it sets the standard for the entire work culture.

PREVENTING DIGITAL OVERLOAD AMONG YOUNG EMPLOYEES

Encourage Using Productivity Apps

Smartphones aren't only for scrolling through countless social content or messaging friends; they can also be used to assist with work. There are countless time management apps that can help you use a smartphone effectively. It's almost impossible to tell Gen Z employees to gather their phones in one place where they won't have access to them for the whole day. Instead, encourage them to install productivity apps on their phones to minimize digital distractions. There are productivity apps that allow users to disable notifications and lock the screen so that users aren't picking up their phone every time it makes a noise.

Build Self-Awareness Around Unproductive Digital Habits

Younger employees know how to use digital tools, but there are still a few who aren't aware that prolonged digital use can be unproductive. As a leader, you can encourage them to reflect on their digital habits—are they using smartphones to assist their work? Building self-awareness around unproductive digital habits, such as excessive social media use or constantly checking messages, will allow them to take proactive steps in managing their digital use.

Create Quiet Spaces

Designated quiet spaces can help employees retreat to refocus without digital distractions. You can try to implement quiet zones where digital devices are prohibited. These spaces should provide a physical and mental break from digital noises, allowing employees to regain concentration.

Encourage Social Connections

A strong social connection between employees can minimize digital distractions. In the workplace, I like to encourage team-building activities, especially physical ones, to create a supportive work environment. These activities can act as a buffer for digital overload.

Suggest Reasonable Parameters Around Responding to Messages During Off-Work Hours

Ideally, there should be clear boundaries between work hours and off-work hours. However, there are some cases where work-related communications may happen outside of work hours. When this happens, you need to set clear expectations and policies regarding communicating outside of regular working hours, such as after 9 p.m. or during the weekends. You can encourage employees to establish reasonable parameters for responding to messages during off-work hours. Such as expected late responses or no responses at all until working hours begin. This promotes a healthy work-life balance and overall digital wellness.

Avoiding Off-Hour Communications

As a professional team, I usually discourage off-hour communications unless absolutely necessary. This habit creates a culture that respects personal time and emphasizes the importance of time efficiency.

ENCOURAGING DEEP WORK

Psychologists Mihaly Csikszentmihalyi and Jeanne Nakamura (2004), in their TED Talk, popularized the concept of the "flow state," also known as "being in the zone." They explained that when individuals are "in the zone" of the task at hand, they feel the utmost involvement and focus, and are immersed in the work they are doing. They might not realize how much time has passed, think about anything else, or be able to judge their performance. This positive psychological state boosts someone's productivity to its highest level. So, how does one achieve this flow?

Statistics suggest that between 15-20% of adults struggle with procrastination (Shatz, n.d.). The causes vary, from a lack of enjoyment in the task to improper time management. In my experience, many young employees struggle with bad time management, leading to procrastination. If we can find a solution to fix this bad time management habit, I believe it would be easier to reach the flow state.

Let's talk about how to encourage deep work in the workplace and utilize digital tools to practice effective time management.

Tools and Practices for Effective Time Management

Time Tracking Tools

- Time Doctor

Time Doctor is a time-tracking app designed to help individuals or teams manage their working time effectively. It's particularly useful for self-employed workers and freelancers who need to track their work hours accurately. This app allows users to track the time spent on their tasks and it can also create and manage different tasks, helping users to organize their work. What's unique about this app is that it can monitor the websites and applications the users access during work hours, helping users identify potential distractions and eliminate them.

- Toggl

Similar to Time Doctor, Toggl is a popular time-tracking app. Users can organize their tasks by associating time entries with specific projects, helping to track time for different projects separately. The app also provides detailed reports on time usage, progress, and productivity. This can provide useful insight into how time is allocated across different activities.

- TMetric

TMetric is a time-tracking app that enables users to gain insights into their personal or team productivity. It can detect periods of inactivity, giving users insights into how effectively their time is utilized. It also assists in tracking billable hours, making it easier for freelancers and businesses to generate accurate invoices based on the amount of working hours spent on a task.

Task Management Tools

- Asana

Asana allows your team to manage projects together, making it easy for team-based work. It's suitable for both small teams and large enterprises. The collaborative structure helps team members separate tasks into manageable components, which is helpful in tracking progress. A unique feature that this app has is the timeline view, where team members can visualize plans and deadlines to provide a clear timeline of the project and potential obstacles.

- Trello

Trello is an app designed to simplify team project management. Similar to Asana, Trello allows users to categorize tasks in a kanban board, where each task is visually represented on a board and moves through different stages as the project progresses. This app's unique feature is the card-based system, where each card represents a task and can include detailed information, due dates, and comments from other team members.

- Todoist

Todoist is an intuitive platform for organizing team projects. It's available on desktop and mobile devices, allowing users to access their work anywhere. Its unique feature is the natural language input, in which users can add tasks using plain language, and Todoist will automatically interpret details, such as due dates and main priorities based on the language input.

- Jira

Jira is an app designed for managing collaborative projects. This app excels at issue tracking, allowing teams to prioritize and track specific tasks, bugs, and other project-related problems. Each issue can be assigned a variety of attributes, such as the status, the priority, and who will be assigned to resolve it. One of the unique features of Jira is its customizable workflows, allowing each team member to define their own workflows, ensuring that Jira adapts to the team's preferred way of working.

Productivity Methods

- Pomodoro

Pomodoro, meaning "tomato" in Italian, is a popular time management technique developed by Francesco Cirillo who was inspired to break down tasks using his tomato-shaped kitchen timer. The Pomodoro technique involves focusing on a task for 25 to 50 minutes, then resting for 5 to 10 minutes before going back to work again. This technique proves to be effective for deep-focusing and allowing rest to recharge again. Personally, I find this technique is effective. In one hour, I am able to complete more focused work with the 25-minute work and five-minute rest interval.

- Time-blocking

Time-blocking is a personal time management technique in which specific tasks are scheduled in small segments, typically per day or per week. This technique is useful if you want a detailed time management strategy, focusing on allocating dedicated time periods for specific tasks to help you stay organized.

Avoid Distractions

Distractions aren't limited to just smartphones; any tools that aren't related to work should be eliminated. Make sure to avoid things that are potentially distracting, such as television. To improve focus, it is important to work in a clean, conducive, and comfortable space.

Take Breaks

Taking breaks is the key to maintaining focus. You can't expect to work nonstop for hours as your body needs rest to recharge. During work hours, I usually set a timer for a few minutes to rest my eyes, take a walk, or regain focus. This method is especially useful if you're working in front of a computer.

DIGITAL DETOX

A poll conducted by Common Sense Media (n.d.) revealed that around 50% of teens admit they feel addicted to mobile phones, and around 78% of teens said that they check digital devices hourly. These numbers are clear evidence that digital addiction can disrupt our daily lives. We often forget what is happening in front of us due to our prolonged focus on our mobile phones. This is why we need a digital detox.

A digital detox is a method to reduce screen time and distance ourselves from digital devices, at least for a period of time. This helps us focus on the present moment and immerse ourselves in our surroundings.

Benefits

Reduced Stress and Anxiety

Excessive digital usage also affects our mental health. A study by George et al. (2017) revealed that heavy technology use was associated with increased mental health problems among adolescents. Using technology in moderation can reduce stress and anxiety as it helps us to be more engaged with the physical environment rather than the things that are happening in the virtual realm.

Improved Sleep Quality

Studies suggest that digital use before bedtime decreases sleep quality. The blue light that digital screens emit suppresses the production of melatonin, a hormone that makes us sleepy (Newsom & Singh, 2024.) By taking a break from digital use, we reduce this exposure to blue light, allowing our bodies to naturally regulate healthy sleep–wake cycles.

Increased Productivity and Focus

When sleep quality increases, so do concentration and productivity. Taking a break from digital use also minimizes the tendency to switch between tasks that potentially scatter our focus.

More Time for Self-Care and Relationships

Digital detoxing provides an opportunity for self-reflection, allowing you to be more in tune with your intuition, emotions, and feelings. This will create an opportunity to genuinely understand how you can be present with the people you love by spending quality time with them and deepening your connections with them.

Why It's Especially Important for Young Employees

Young people often face the pressure to be constantly connected with their digital lives, and digital detox allows them to take a break and recharge, promoting better mental health. In the digital age, young employees may find it challenging to establish clear boundaries between their work and personal life, as digital use is almost fully integrated in professional settings. This is why a digital detox is important as it helps to create a healthier work-life balance for young employees.

SUMMARY

In this digital era, we often forget to balance our attention between our digital and physical lives. In the workplace, managing digital distractions and digital detoxing are especially important for young employees as they tend to be heavy technology users. Practicing the methods I've outlined in this chapter serves as a reminder to reclaim moments of mindfulness, self-care, and deeper connections with loved ones. It's a conscious decision to shift our focus to the present moment, fostering a balance between the digital and physical aspects of our lives.

In the next chapter, you will learn how to get ready to adapt to the evolution of the workforce, led by Gen Z individuals.

Chapter Ten

ADAPTING TO CHANGE–THE FUTURE OF WORK

I t's true that change is the only constant in life, and in no other area is this truer than in the Gen Z-led workplace of the future. As the next generation takes the reins, traditional work structures and practices are being reimagined and reshaped. Gen Z, known for their tech-savviness and entrepreneurial spirit, is driving a shift towards remote work, flexible schedules, and a greater emphasis on work-life balance. With their fresh perspectives and innovative ideas, Gen Z is challenging the status quo and pushing for a more inclusive and diverse work environment. The workplace of the future will be dynamic, adaptable, and driven by the values and aspirations of this generation.

This revolution in the workplace is going to be quick and widespread, and business leaders have to be ready for it. In this chapter, I want to guide you on how to prepare for and adapt to the future of the workforce. I encourage you to share the knowledge that you have gained from this book so everyone can contribute to a future-ready organization.

PREPARING FOR EVOLVING WORK DYNAMICS

Embrace Flexibility

According to a survey, 72% of Gen Z employees expressed their inclination to leave or contemplate leaving a job if their employer fails to provide a flexible work policy (Noor, 2023.) This statistic highlights the growing importance of work-life balance and the desire for greater autonomy among the younger generation. The future of the workforce may be even more flexible and give employees more control over how they want to approach their work. I can guarantee that a flexible work culture will help businesses attract new talent and stand out in the tight labor market.

Invest in Reskilling and Upskilling

Technology continues to evolve, and Gen Zs need the skills to continuously adapt. Investing in upskilling programs is essential to keep employees—especially the younger ones—relevant in the workforce. This commitment will encourage younger employees to continuously learn and ensure that your team is equipped with the necessary skills to tackle future challenges.

Rethink the Employee Experience

Employees are more than tools to create profit; they are individuals with unique talents, aspirations, and needs, whose well-being and fulfillment contribute to the success of the organization. As a leader, it's your duty to foster a positive employee experience. Focus on team collaboration, build a supportive company culture, promote their well-being, and constantly update policies to fit new ways of working.

Leverage Artificial Intelligence and Automation

Artificial Intelligence (AI) is slowly integrating into the workforce. This new form of automation can significantly alter the workforce as it generally enhances workers' efficiency and productivity. From generating texts and images to brainstorming prompts, AI is a valuable tool that you can use to leverage your organization's success. You can use AI to empower employees by automating routine tasks and allowing them to be more strategic in decision-making. The future of the workforce will most probably successfully integrate these technologies with a thoughtful approach, balancing digital automation with a human touch.

Link Talent and Business Strategy

Aligning your team's talents with business strategies is crucial for success. You need to be proactive in understanding the competence of your employees, especially the younger ones, as they have the energy for innovation.

A WORD OF CAUTION

As you move forward, there are potential drawbacks if you cater too heavily to Gen Z's workplace needs. The key is to find balance and always look for win-win solutions. What are these potential obstacles?

Alienating Other Generations

An overemphasis on Gen Z preferences may result in the alienation of older employees. You must be careful not to neglect the needs and expectations of older generations, such as Gen X and Boomers. If you cater too highly to Gen Z's needs, it can lead to feelings of exclusion, which could potentially create more conflicts.

Difficulties Retaining Some Gen Z Employees

The truth is, no Gen Z is the same as the other. They are a dynamic generation and they are in a state of constant change. These rapid changes pose challenges in retaining some employees. They might find a new interest or passion or suddenly want to shift career progressions. Whichever the case, you likely can't fulfill all of their needs; you must simply provide an opportunity for them to have the autonomy they need. Sometimes, the new policies you implement may not align with them, and that is okay.

Burdensome Costs

Implementing new systems may come with significant costs, especially with Gen Z employees. Implementing the latest technology and creating flexible workspaces, training programs, and regular activities can strain financial resources. Your company must carefully weigh the benefits against the costs, ensuring that your investments are worth it.

Loss of Team's Continuity

Frequent changes to accommodate Gen Z preferences may disturb the continuity of established teams. Sometimes, you may need to switch team members, and this rapid shift in team dynamics will affect team cohesion, communication, and overall effectiveness. It's important for you to strike a balance between embracing innovation and maintaining a stable team.

Ongoing Intergenerational Conflicts

Conflicts happen every day, and a multigenerational company may be more prone to them. Clashes between different age groups may arise if there is an imbalance in attention and resources. Be aware of internal politics and cross-generational collaboration. This is why open communication is important as it gives you an opportunity to address these conflicts peacefully.

SUMMARY

As we conclude the last chapter, you are now ready to embark on an exciting journey to witness the change of a Gen Z-led workforce. The transformation ahead promises innovation, dynamism, and a fresh perspective within the workplace. However, as with any significant shift, it's crucial to approach this evolution with care.

While meeting the demands of Gen Z is critical, our exploration has shown a few obstacles that must be carefully navigated. Balancing innovation and stability, promoting inclusivity across generations, adopting effective retention tactics, managing expenses wisely, and keeping team continuity are all critical to the success of this transition.

Remember, the objective is to maintain a balance, to create a workplace that not only appeals to Gen Z preferences but also meets the different demands of other generations. By doing so, your team can fully realize the potential of a multigenerational workforce, encouraging cooperation, creativity, and long-term success.

CONCLUSION

My journey in understanding the complex characteristics of Gen Z in the workplace has been an eye-opener. I hope you feel the same as we conclude this book. The exploration of Gen Z's values, preferences, and dynamics has revealed a uniqueness that significantly shapes the future of the workforce.

As we wrap up this insightful journey, it's evident that Gen Z brings a wealth of innovation, creativity, and technological fluency as well as a commitment to social justice. However, there will be potential challenges ahead, and I hope I have adequately equipped you to acknowledge the nuances associated with integrating a multigenerational team in your organization.

The journey has shed light on the relationship between technology and human connection. While Gen Z is sometimes referred to as the "digital generation," it is critical to acknowledge the human element that coexists with their technological capability. The desire for meaningful connections, purposeful employment, and a sense of belonging remains an essential driving force for this age. Organizations that can achieve a balance between technology and humans are better positioned to attract, retain, and maximize Gen Z talent.

It is critical to underline the continuous nature of this generation. The workplace is a dynamic environment, and understanding generational dynamics is an ongoing process. The features and attributes we associate with Gen Z today may shift as they advance in their careers, and staying aware of these changes is critical for companies seeking a prosperous future.

In terms of diversity and inclusion, I emphasized the necessity of building environments that value differences. The workplace is getting increasingly diverse in terms of age, cultural backgrounds, beliefs, and experiences. Embracing diversity is more than simply a societal expectation; it is a strategic priority for developing creativity, innovation, and resilience inside organizations.

Navigating the path ahead requires an inclusive approach, one that challenges conventional means. You must be ready to embrace change while at the same time recognizing the importance of your team's continuity and fostering a workplace culture that values diversity. I hope the lessons learned from this book will serve as a guide to harness the full potential of Gen Z's strengths.

In the ever-evolving landscape of the workforce, adaptability is key. By appreciating the distinctive qualities of your Gen Z employees, you will know how to manage them better. You will no longer label them as difficult to work with, lazy, or disobedient; instead, you will see them as opportunities to improve yourself as a leader.

You will now be better able to understand them, recognize their values, and appreciate their ideas. This in turn will help you master concise and visually-focused communication and how to adapt your leadership style in the digital age.

As you apply the insights you have gained from this book, I hope your organization thrives in the era of a Gen Z-led workforce. Now that you have the tools and insights to improve how you interact with Generation Z in the workplace, don't wait for change to happen; be the catalyst!

Challenge yourself to implement at least one strategy from each chapter of this book within a month. Whether it's about balancing digital integration, improving communication across all platforms, or encouraging team innovation, your initiative will benefit not only the young team members but the entire organization in the long run.

I appreciate you taking the time to explore the complexities of Gen Z in the workplace with me. Your feedback and ideas on the content is appreciated, so please feel free to offer your thoughts on the book at any time. Thank you for taking part in this adventure.

REFERENCES

Apostol, R. (2023, October 26). Nine wellness initiatives to engage Gen Zers in the workplace. *Vantage Fit Blog.* https://www.vantagefit.io/blog/well ness-initiatives-to-attract-gen-zers/

Assertive communication skills for managers. (n.d.). *Pryor Learning.* https:// www.pryor.com/training-webinars/assertive-communication-skills-for-managers/

Atchison, J. (2021, January 8). Council post: Four ways to create transparency in the workplace. *Forbes.* https://www.forbes.com/sites/theyec/2021/ 01/08/four-ways-to-create-transparency-in-the-workplace/?sh= 6c3f67de7ff6

Baby Boomer: Definition, age range, characteristics, and impact. (2023, July 25). *Investopedia.* https://www.investopedia.com/terms/b/baby_ boomer.asp

Badgujar, V. (2022, February 4). 12 time management tools and techniques that actually work. *Time Doctor Blog.* https://www.timedoctor.com/blog/ time-management-tools-and-techniques/

Baird, B., Smallwood, J., Mrazek, M. D., Kam, J. W. Y., Franklin, M. S., & Schooler, J. W. (2012, August 31). Inspired by distraction: Mind wandering facilitates creative incubation. *Psychological Science, 23*(10), 1117–1122. https://doi.org/10.1177/0956797612446024

Beranek, C. (2023, April 20). The importance of face-to-face communication in a digital world. *Entrepreneur.* https://www.entrepreneur.com/leader ship/the-importance-of-face-to-face-communication-in-a-digital/449550

Birditt, K. S., Fingerman, K. L., & Almeida, D. M. (2005). Age differences in exposure and reactions to interpersonal tensions: A daily diary study. *Psychology and Aging, 20*(2), 330–340. https://doi.org/10.1037/0882-7974. 20.2.330

Birt, J. (2023, February 3). 7 key benefits of face-to-face communication at work. *Indeed Career Guide.* https://www.indeed.com/career-advice/ career-development/face-to-face-communication

Blanche, A., & Goff-Dupont, S. (2022, January 13). How to navigate your coworkers' communication styles. *Atlassian.* https://www.atlassian.com/ blog/teamwork/how-to-navigate-diverse-communication-styles-at-work

Bredbenner, J. (2020). Generation Z: A study of its workplace communication behaviors and future preferences [Masters thesis, Wichita State

Univeristy]. https://soar.wichita.edu/server/api/core/bitstreams/917b5252-e192-4a88-acac-9f6ab3854ce9/content

British Heart Foundation. (2018, May 14). 10 tips for active listening. *Heart Matters*. https://www.bhf.org.uk/informationsupport/heart-matters-magazine/wellbeing/how-to-talk-about-health-problems/active-listening

Buckner, L. (2023, May 28). How to conduct an effective assessment for employees. *Indeed Career Guide*. https://www.indeed.com/career-advice/career-development/assessment-for-employees

Burns, C. (2023, April 24). Speak Gen Z: How to effectively communicate with the newest generation in the workplace. *Trending Northwest*. https://trendingnorthwest.com/work/communicate-with-generation-z-effectively/

Causes and effects of poor communication in the workplace. (2023, September 26). *TriNet*. https://www.trinet.com/insights/poor-communication/

Chaudhuri, S. (n.d.). *33 best appreciation messages for employee recognition*. Hifives. https://www.hifives.in/best-appreciation-messages-for-employee-recognition/

Chanoine, J.-M. (2023, September 20). Council post: Managing Gen Z: Aligning personal growth with organizational purpose. *Forbes*. https://www.forbes.com/sites/forbesbusinessdevelopmentcouncil/2023/09/20/managing-gen-z-aligning-personal-growth-with-organizational-purpose/?sh=197113292707

Cherry, K. (2020, November 19). The benefits of doing a digital detox. *Verywell Mind*. https://www.verywellmind.com/why-and-how-to-do-a-digital-detox-4771321

Clark, S. (2022, August 1). What does Gen Z really want from brands? *CMSWire*. https://www.cmswire.com/customer-experience/do-your-brands-values-align-with-those-of-gen-z/

Collins, T. (2023, September 14). Is Gen Z sad? Study shows they're more open about struggles with mental health. *USA Today*. https://www.usatoday.com/story/news/nation/2023/09/14/gen-z-open-about-mental-health/70853469007/

Common Sense Media. (n.d.). Dealing with devices: The parent-teen dynamic. https://www.commonsensemedia.org/technology-addiction-concern-controversy-and-finding-balance-infographic

Continuous feedback loop strategies: Top ways to increase engagement. (2022, May 6). *Workleap*. https://workleap.com/blog/continuous-feedback-loop

Cooks-Campbell, A. (2022, August 29). Transparency in the workplace: What it is (and what to avoid). *BetterUp.* https://www.betterup.com/blog/transparency-in-the-workplace

Csikszentmihalyi, M., Nakamura, J. (2004, February). *Flow, the secret to happiness* [Video]. TED Conferences. https://www.ted.com/talks/mihaly_csikszentmihalyi_flow_the_secret_to_happiness

Cuadra, D. (2023, March 15). 16 workplace fears, according to every generation. *Employee Benefit News.* https://www.benefitnews.com/list/workplace-fears-according-to-every-generation

Dagostino, A. (2021, August 9). Council post: Here is how Gen Z is changing the way we communicate. *Forbes.* https://www.forbes.com/sites/forbescommunicationscouncil/2021/08/09/here-is-how-gen-z-is-changing-the-way-we-communicate/?sh=133cc7fe1350

Davis, S. (2020, September 2). What are some examples of visual communication? *Powtoon Blog.* https://www.powtoon.com/blog/examples-of-visual-communication/

De Witte, M. (2022, January 3). What to know about Gen Z. *Stanford News.* https://news.stanford.edu/2022/01/03/know-gen-z/

Deborah. (2022, April 4). How to help your team combat digital distractions at work. *Let's Roam.* https://www.letsroam.com/team-building/resources/technology-distraction-in-the-workplace/

DeLoach, J. (2023, October 25). The evolution of work: How can companies prepare for what's to come? *Corporate Compliance Insights.* https://www.corporatecomplianceinsights.com/evolution-work-companies-prepare/

Dey, P. (2022, December 15). Bridge the multigenerational skill gaps with mentoring. *Mentoring Complete.* https://www.mentoringcomplete.com/bridge-the-multigenerational-skill-gaps-with-mentoring/

Donnelly, L. (2022, August 9). Ten things everyone gets wrong about Gen Z. *Voxburner.* https://www.voxburner.com/blog/facts-about-gen-z/

Douglas, E. (2015, August 25). Communication styles: How to identify communication styles. *Straight Talk.* https://communicationstyles.org/how-to-identify-communication-styles/

Elevate Corporate Training. (2019, April 8). Seven strategies the best leaders use to give feedback. https://www.elevatecorporatetraining.com.au/2019/04/09/7-strategies-good-leaders-can-use-to-give-feedback/

Ezell, D. (2021, May 24). How to use visual communication (and why it matters). *The TechSmith.* https://www.techsmith.com/blog/why-visual-communication-matters/#why

Fey, T. (Writer), Siegal, J. (Writer), Morgan, D. (Writer) & Riggi, J. (Director). (2012, February 16). The Tuxedo Begins (Season 6, Episode 8) [TV Series Episode]. In R. Carlock, T. Fey, M. Klein, L. Michaels, D. Miner, J.

Richmond, J. Riggi (Executive Producers), *30 Rock*. Broadway Video; Little Stranger; NBC Studios; Universal Television.

Fischer, B. (2022, November 10). How to measure innovation in five steps. *Elmhurst University*. https://www.elmhurst.edu/blog/how-to-measure-innovation/

5 social causes for Gen Z in 2023. (2023, August 21). JobTeaser. https://www.jobteaser.com/en/corporate/gen-z-lab/5-social-causes-for-genz-in-2023

14 examples where in-person communication is better than virtual at work. (2022, July 25). *Forbes*. https://www.forbes.com/sites/forbescoachescouncil/2023/01/17/15-ways-leaders-can-effectively-manage-gen-z-workers/?sh=13406c2f4172

Francis, T., & Hoefel, F. (2018). "True Gen": Generation Z and its implications for companies. *McKinsey & Company*. https://shorturl.at/sxABX

Freedman, M. (2023, February 21). What Generation Z wants in their jobs and work. *Business News Daily*. https://www.businessnewsdaily.com/11296-what-gen-z-workers-want.html

Ganesh, K. (2023, June 26). Problems with Gen Z in the workplace. *CultureMonkey*. https://www.culturemonkey.io/employee-engagement/problems-with-gen-z-in-the-workplace/

Geiger, A. W., & Graf, N. (2019, September 5). About one-in-five U.S. adults know someone who goes by a gender-neutral pronoun. *Pew Research Center*. https://www.pewresearch.org/short-reads/2019/09/05/gender-neutral-pronouns/

Generational differences in the workplace: Managing a multi-generational workforce. (2023, June 28). *PayChex*. https://www.paychex.com/articles/human-resources/how-to-manage-multiple-generations-in-the-workplace

Gen Z is defining the future of work – on their own terms, reveals morning consult and Samsung survey. (2023, December 19). *Samsung Newsroom US*. https://news.samsung.com/us/gen-z-defining-future-work-own-terms-reveals-morning-consult-samsung-survey/

George, M. J., Russell, M. A., Piontak, J. R., & Odgers, C. L. (2017, May 3). Concurrent and subsequent associations between daily digital technology use and high-risk adolescents' mental health symptoms. *Child Development, 89*(1), 78–88. https://doi.org/10.1111/cdev.12819

Gikonyo, G (2022, November 4). Gen Z: Understanding the "I do me" generation. *The Standard*. https://www.standardmedia.co.ke/entertainment/features/article/2001459758/gen-z-understanding-the-i-do-me-generation

Grossman, D. (2021, November 6). Employees' digital overload and what you can do about it. *The Grossman Group*. https://www.yourthoughtpartner.com/blog/employees-digital-overload-and-what-you-can-do-about-it

Grossman, D. (2023, May 1). 17 communication channels for engaging busy employees. *The Grossman Group.* https://www.yourthoughtpartner.com/blog/communication-channels

Harrell, C. (2023, March 20). Seven Gen Z trends that are quickly changing the world. *Brainz Magazine.* https://www.brainzmagazine.com/post/7-gen-z-trends-that-are-quickly-changing-the-world#:

Harris, Y. (2023, August 16). Communication styles in the workplace: Gen Z, Boomer and beyond. *Powell Software.* https://powell-software.com/resources/blog/communication-styles/

Hart, J. (2023, September 1). Managers say Gen Zers aren't getting work done and lack basic social skills – and it's driving them crazy. *Business Insider.* https://www.businessinsider.com/managers-speak-out-about-experiences-with-gen-z-employees-2023-8

Hassell, D. (2013, July 18). Nine ways to give effective employee feedback. *15Five.* https://www.15five.com/blog/9-ways-to-give-effective-employee-feedback/

Hastwell, C. (2023, January 18). Engaging and managing a multigenerational workforce. *Great Place to Work.* https://www.greatplacetowork.com/resources/blog/engaging-and-managing-multigenerational-workforce

Haycox, S. (2022, June 17). Five tips for communicating with Gen Z employees. *Interact Software.* https://www.interactsoftware.com/blog/tips-for-communicating-with-gen-z-employees/

Henderson, L. (2022, May 19). Ten time management tools and techniques for best results. *Nifty.* https://niftypm.com/blog/time-management-tools-and-techniques/

Hoory, L. (2023, March 8). The state of workplace communication in 2023. *Forbes.* https://www.forbes.com/advisor/business/digital-communication-workplace/

How do you measure and reward creativity and innovation in your organization? (n.d.). *LinkedIn.* https://www.linkedin.com/advice/1/how-do-you-measure-reward-creativity-innovation-1c

How Gen Z is shaping the future of technology (2023, May 5). *Amber Blog.* https://amberstudent.com/blog/post/how-gen-z-is-shaping-the-future-of-technology

How Gen Z is shaping the future of technology. (n.d.). *Shockoe.* https://shockoe.com/ideas/design-and-innovation/how-gen-z-is-shaping-the-future-of-technology/

Hurt, K., & Dye, D. (2020, July 13). The main reasons employees don't speak their mind at work. *Fast Company.* https://www.fastcompany.com/90526638/the-main-reasons-employees-dont-speak-their-mind-at-work

Imagery vs text. Which does the brain prefer? (n.d.). World of Learning. https://

www.learnevents.com/learning-insights/imagery-vs-text-which-does-the-brain-prefer/

Indeed Editorial Team. (2023, February 3). How to effectively use active listening in the workplace. *Indeed Career Guide.* https://www.indeed.com/career-advice/career-development/listening-in-the-workplace

Indeed Editorial Team. (20221, June 24). 13 needs of employees and how to meet them. *Indeed Career Guide.* https://www.indeed.com/career-advice/career-development/needs-of-employees

Irvine, M. (2023, August 1). What is the biggest misconception of Gen Z in the workplace? *LinkedIn.* https://www.linkedin.com/business/talent/blog/learning-and-development/what-is-biggest-misconception-of-gen-z-in-workplace

Jahns, K. (2021, August 10). The environment is Gen Z's no. 1 concern – and some companies are taking advantage of that. *CNBC.* https://www.cnbc.com/2021/08/10/the-environment-is-gen-zs-no-1-concern-but-beware-of-greenwashing.html

Jha, M. (2020, March 23). Communicating with Generation Z in the workplace. *ContactMonkey.* https://www.contactmonkey.com/blog/gen-z-employees

Kam, J. W. Y., Irving, Z. C., Mills, C., Patel, S., Gopnik, A., & Knight, R. T. (2021). Distinct electrophysiological signatures of task-unrelated and dynamic thoughts. *Proceedings of the National Academy of Sciences of the United States of America, 118*(4). https://doi.org/10.1073/pnas.2011796118

Kane, K. (n.d.). Unpacking a generation: Gen Z holds two truths at once. *Eggstrategy.* https://eggstrategy.com/unpacking-a-generation/

Kelley, K. (n.d.). How do you foster a culture of open and honest communication in your organization? *LinkedIn.* https://www.linkedin.com/advice/0/how-do-you-foster-culture-open-honest-communication

Kelly, J. (2023, July 31). Gen Z is labeled as "difficult" in the workplace, but there's more to the story. *Forbes.* https://www.forbes.com/sites/jackkelly/2023/07/31/gen-z-is-labeled-as-difficult-in-the-workplace-but-theres-more-to-the-story/?sh=30b96c2a7d7f

Kerner, S. M. (2023, March). *Corporate social responsibility (CSR).* TechTarget. https://www.techtarget.com/searchcio/definition/corporate-social-responsibility-CSR#:

Key performance indicator (KPI): Definition, examples & types. (n.d.). Klipfolio. https://www.klipfolio.com/resources/articles/what-is-a-key-performance-indicator#:

Kher, R., Purohit, P., & Jain, S. (n.d.). What are some effective ways for leaders to create a positive work environment? *LinkedIn.* https://www.linkedin.com/advice/1/what-some-effective-ways-leaders-create-posi

tive

King, M. P. (2023, October 6). Gen Z's biggest skills gap that is fueling their social anxiety at work: Managing ambiguity. *Fortune.* https://fortune.com/2023/10/06/gen-z-biggest-skills-gap-social-anxiety-work-managing-ambiguity-michelle-king/

Koepsell, L. (2020, February 10). Gen Z "stans" feedback - here's how to structure it best. *The Washington Center.* https://resources.twc.edu/articles/gen-z-stans-feedback-heres-how-to-structure-it-best#:

Korn Ferry. (2018, March 12). Millennials as bosses: Forget face-to-face, online messaging new norm for communicating with direct reports, according to Korn Ferry survey. *BusinessWire.* https://www.businesswire.com/news/home/20180312005112/en/Millennials-Bosses-Forget-Face-to-Face-Online-Messaging-New

Krumrie, M. (2019, September 19). How to answer three job interview questions about communication style. *FlexJobs.* https://www.flexjobs.com/blog/post/answer-job-interview-questions-communication-style-v2/

Kulshreshtha, A (2022, September 12). *Career opportunities in visual communication.* Indian Institute of Art & Design. https://www.iiad.edu.in/the-circle/career-opportunities-in-visual-communication/

Kumar, V. (2023, April 18). Gen Z in the workplace: How should companies adapt? *Johns Hopkins University.* https://imagine.jhu.edu/blog/2023/04/18/gen-z-in-the-workplace-how-should-companies-adapt/

Lambert, A. (2020, December 11). Recognizing the basic needs of the individuals in your team. *LinkedIn.* https://www.linkedin.com/pulse/recognizing-basic-needs-individuals-your-team-alan-lambert/

Larralde, A. (2022, October 28). A practical guide to continuous feedback at work. *Betterworks.* https://www.betterworks.com/magazine/continuous-feedback/

Lau, G. (2022, May 8). Four workplace communication styles (and how to approach them). *Hypercontext.* https://hypercontext.com/blog/communication/workplace-communication-styles

Lifespan Blog Team. (2023, June 8). What is a digital detox and do you need one? *Lifespan.* https://www.lifespan.org/lifespan-living/what-digital-detox-and-do-you-need-one

Long, B. (2022, October 12). Transparency in the workplace: Everything you need to know. *Insight Global.* https://insightglobal.com/blog/transparency-in-the-workplace/

Lupis, J. C. (2016, June 28). Almost half of America's Gen Z population belongs to a minority group. *Marketing Charts.* https://www.marketingcharts.com/demographics-and-audiences-68603

Maier-Liu, L. (2011, July 6). 20 tips for managing young employees. *ERC.*

https://yourerc.com/blog/20-tips-for-managing-young-employees/

Maurer, R. (2019, November 7). How to reduce digital distractions at work. *SHRM Foundation.* https://www.shrm.org/topics-tools/news/technol ogy/how-to-reduce-digital-distractions-work

McLaren, S. (2019, October 8). Six Gen Z traits you need to know to attract, hire, and retain them. *LinkedIn.* https://www.linkedin.com/business/ talent/blog/talent-acquisition/how-to-hire-and-retain-generation-z

McMillan, R. L., Kaufman, S. B., & Singer, J. L. (2013, September 23). Ode to positive constructive daydreaming. *Frontiers in Psychology, 4.* https://doi. org/10.3389/fpsyg.2013.00626

Medaris, A. (2023, November 1). *Gen Z adults and younger millennials are "completely overwhelmed" by stress.* American Psychological Association. https://www.apa.org/topics/stress/generation-z-millennials-young-adults-worries

Meola, A. (2023, January 1). Generation Z news: Latest characteristics, research, and facts. *Insider Intelligence.* https://www.insiderintelligence. com/insights/generation-z-facts/

Microsoft. (2021, July 27). Five reasons to use visual aids for speeches and presentations. *Microsoft 365.* https://www.microsoft.com/en-us/ microsoft-365-life-hacks/presentations/five-reasons-to-use-visual-aids-for-speeches-and-presentations

Mind Tools. (2022). Active listening. https://www.mindtools.com/az4wxv7/ active-listening

Mirbabaie, M., Stieglitz, S., & Marx, J. (2022). Digital detox. *Business & Information Systems Engineering.* https://doi.org/10.1007/s12599-022-00747-x

Moore, K. (2014, December 4). Giving S.M.A.R.T. feedback to Millennials. *Forbes.* https://www.forbes.com/sites/karlmoore/2014/12/04/giving-s-m-a-r-t-feedback-to-millennials/?sh=5afb94f571d3

Mostert, N.M. (2008, December). *How to measure creativity on eight different levels in your organization.* Mostert Consultancy for Creativity and Innovation Management. https://mccim.nl/publications/how-to-measure-creativity.pdf

Motivation theories: Individual needs. (2015). *CliffNotes.* https://www.cliffs notes.com/study-guides/principles-of-management/motivating-and-rewarding-employees/motivation-theories-individual-needs

Naidu, K. (2023, June 15). Decoding Gen Z: Highly individualistic and low on regrets - this generation has what it takes. *Business Insider.* https://www. businessinsider.in/thelife/news/decoding-genz-highly-individualistic-and-low-on-regrets-this-generation-has-what-it-takes/articleshow/ 101011641.cms

Nallalingham, L. (2023, September 9). Open communication: Fostering a culture of feedback. *LinkedIn.* https://www.linkedin.com/pulse/open-communication-fostering-culture-feedback-lee-nallalingham/

Navigating identity and embracing change: The Gen Z journey. (n.d.). *LinkedIn.* https://www.linkedin.com/pulse/navigating-identity-embracing-change-gen-z-journey-vishwajeet-singh/

Nawrat, A. (2022, August 11). It's not all about salaries for Gen Z. *UNLEASH.* https://www.unleash.ai/compensation-and-benefits/its-not-all-about-salaries-for-gen-z/

Newsom, R., Singh A. (2024, January 12). Blue light: what it is and how it affects sleep. *Sleep Foundation.* https://www.sleepfoundation.org/bedroom-environment/blue-light

Nishadha. (2018, October 9). Five amazing advantages of visual communication you can't ignore. *Creately Blog.* https://creately.com/blog/diagrams/visual-communication-benefits/

Noor, A. (2023, September 13). 20+ Gen Z statistics for employers in 2023. *Qureos Hiring Guide.* https://www.qureos.com/hiring-guide/gen-z-statistics#:

Notre Dame of Maryland University. (2019, February 6). *The evolution of communication from Boomers to Gen Z.* https://online.ndm.edu/news/communication/evolution-of-communication/

O'Donnel, L. (2020, July 17). Managers: Are you building a culture of trust? *Great Place to Work.* https://www.greatplacetowork.com/resources/blog/managers-are-you-building-a-culture-of-trust

Ochis, K. (2023, October 11). Council post: Five ways to work well with Gen Z employees. *Forbes.* https://www.forbes.com/sites/forbescoachescouncil/2023/10/11/five-ways-to-work-well-with-gen-z-employees/?sh=4d6066102a58

Parker, K., & Igielnik, R. (2020, May 14). On the cusp of adulthood and facing an uncertain future: What we know about Gen Z so far. *Pew Research Center.* https://www.pewresearch.org/social-trends/2020/05/14/on-the-cusp-of-adulthood-and-facing-an-uncertain-future-what-we-know-about-gen-z-so-far-2/

Paulyne. (2023, February 14). Gen Z and work-life balance: Essential tips to better understand this generation. *deskbird.* https://www.deskbird.com/blog/gen-z-work-life-balance

Pelta, R. (2019, September 28). Workplace distractions reduce employee productivity. *FlexJobs.* https://www.flexjobs.com/blog/post/workplace-distractions-types/

Perna, M. C. (2020, July 15). How a technology detox can save you from burnout. *Forbes.* https://www.forbes.com/sites/markcperna/2020/07/

15/how-a-technology-detox-can-save-you-from-burnout/?sh=1871f5872af8

Petrock, V. (2021, November 15). US Generation Z technology and media use. *Insider Intelligence*. https://www.insiderintelligence.com/content/us-generation-z-technology-and-media-use

Phair, S. (2019). Everything marketers need to know about Gen Z: Authenticity with individuality. *Marketing Tech News*. https://www.marketingtechnews.net/news/2019/may/01/everything-marketers-need-know-about-gen-z-authenticity-individuality/

Post-pandemic workforce dynamics, pt. 1: Evolution is an opportunity. (2023, September 15). *Guidehouse*. https://guidehouse.com/insights/mega trends/optimizing-workforce/evolution-of-workforce-management-part-1

The power of feedback: how open communication can improve employee well-being and performance. (n.d.). *Corporate Wellness Magazine*. https://www.corporatewellnessmagazine.com/article/the-power-of-feedback-how-open-communication-can-improve-employee-well-being-and-performance

Prichard, M. (2021, February 4). How to overcome digital overload: Four tips to support your team. *Mac's List*. https://www.macslist.org/for-employ ers/how-to-overcome-digital-overload-4-tips-to-support-your-team

Prodger, B. (2020, September 30). Gen Z's approach to wellbeing. *Stress Matters*. https://stressmatters.org.uk/gen-zs-approach-to-wellbeing/

Rasool, T., Warraich, N. F., & Sajid, M. (2022). Examining the impact of technology overload at the workplace: A systematic review. *SAGE Open, 12*(3), 215824402211143. https://doi.org/10.1177/21582440221114320

Roy, B. D. (2019, February 20). Nine best practices to keep employee satisfaction high. *Vantage Circle HR*. https://blog.vantagecircle.com/employee-satisfaction/

Sam. (2021, November 21). 3 continuous feedback loop strategies in 2024. *Matterapp*. https://matterapp.com/blog/continuous-feedback-loop

Sanders, T. (2023, August 25). Four leadership strategies to build resilience in the face of evolving workforce dynamics. *Quartz*. https://qz.com/4-lead ership-strategies-to-build-resilience-in-the-face-1850770981

Segal, E. (2023, May 24). How Gen Z's impact on the workplace continues to grow. *Forbes*. https://www.forbes.com/sites/edwardsegal/2023/05/24/how-gen-zs-impact-on-the-workplace-continues-to-grow/?sh=266710826a5b

Selig, A. (2023, October 19). Generation influence: Reaching Gen Z in the new digital paradigm. *WP Engine*. https://wpengine.com/resources/gen-z-2020-full-report/#Identity_and_influence

7 key truths about innovating for Generation Z. (n.d.). *Frog.* https://www.frog.co/designmind/7-key-truths-about-innovating-for-generation-z

Shatz, I. (n.d.). Procrastination statistics: Interesting and useful statistics about procrastination. *Solving Procrastination.* https://solvingprocrastination.com/procrastination-statistics/#Statistics_about_procrastinators

Siegel, B. (2023, June 23). Council post: debunking myths about Gen Z workers—and how employers can adapt. *Forbes.* https://www.forbes.com/sites/forbesbusinesscouncil/2023/06/23/debunking-myths-about-gen-z-workers-and-how-employers-can-adapt/?sh=17a958736f53

Sims, G. (2023, June 6). Seven secrets to managing Gen Z in a remote workplace. *Insperity.* https://www.insperity.com/blog/gen-z-in-the-workplace/

Stacey, K. (2022, November 22). How to effectively communicate with Gen Z in the workplace. *Connecteam.* https://connecteam.com/effectively-communicate-gen-z-work/

The state of consumer spending: Gen Z shoppers demand sustainable retail. (n.d.). First Insight. https://www.firstinsight.com/white-papers-posts/gen-z-shoppers-demand-sustainability

Steffens, R. (2018, October 5). 11 visual storytelling techniques you should utilize in your content. *Bluleadz.* https://www.bluleadz.com/blog/11-visual-storytelling-techniques-you-should-be-utilizing-in-your-content

Subbramaniyam, S. (2023, July 12). Practical strategies for fostering a culture of open communication in your organization. *LinkedIn.* linkedin.com/pulse/practical-strategies-fostering-culture-open-communication-sunil-s/

Tansey, C. (2021, June 16). What Is continuous feedback and what are its benefits? *Lattice.* https://lattice.com/library/what-is-continuous-feedback-and-what-are-its-benefits

The Annie E. Casey Foundation. (2011, January 1). From the 2010 census: The changing child population of the United States. https://www.aecf.org/resources/the-changing-child-population-of-the-united-states-2010

The Annie E. Casey Foundation. (2021, January 12). What are the core characteristics of Generation Z? https://www.aecf.org/blog/what-are-the-core-characteristics-of-generation-z

Thomas, M. (2022, July 26). What does work-life balance even mean? *Forbes.* https://www.forbes.com/sites/maurathomas/2022/07/26/what-does-work-life-balance-even-mean/?sh=23ce87252617

3 identities of the Generation Z era: The inventor, artist, entrepreneur. (2023, August 10). *Amber Blog.* https://amberstudent.com/blog/post/identities-of-the-generation-z-era-the-inventor-artist-entrepreneur#:

3 in 4 managers find it difficult to work with Gen Z. (2023, April 17).

ResumeBuilder. https://www.resumebuilder.com/3-in-4-managers-find-it-difficult-to-work-with-genz/

Tidswell, E. (2022, May 13). Does Gen Z care about sustainability? Stats and facts in 2022. *Goodmakertales*. https://goodmakertales.com/does-gen-z-care-about-sustainability/

Tracy, B. (2017, November 15). Time management tools and techniques. *Brian Tracy's Self Improvement & Professional Development Blog*. https://www.briantracy.com/blog/time-management/time-management-tools-and-techniques-time-planner-master-list/

Udemy Business. (2018). *2018 workplace distraction report*. https://research.udemy.com/wp-content/uploads/2018/03/Workplace-Distraction-Report-2018-2021-Rebrand-v3-gs.pdf

Ulster University. (2022). The sustainability generation: Why do Generation Z care about this planet? https://www.ulster.ac.uk/faculties/ulster-university-business-school/updates/other/the-sustainability-generation-why-do-generation-z-care-about-this-planet

Understanding Generation Z in the workplace. (2019, July 3). *Deloitte*. https://www2.deloitte.com/us/en/pages/consumer-business/articles/understanding-generation-z-in-the-workplace.html

UNiDAYS. (2018, November). *Z: A generation redefining health and wellness*. https://p.corporate.myunidays.com/z-a-generation-redefining-health-and-wellness

University of St. Augustine for Health Sciences. (2019, October 3). *Nine popular time management techniques and tools*. https://www.usa.edu/blog/time-management-techniques/

Upton-Clark, E. (2023, May 9). It's official: Gen Z is the hustle generation. *Business Insider*. https://www.businessinsider.com/gen-z-hustle-generation-jobs-work-side-hustle-freelance-2023-5

Urick, M. J., Hollensbe, E. C., Masterson, S. S., & Lyons, S. T. (2016). Understanding and managing intergenerational conflict: An examination of influences and strategies. *Work, Aging and Retirement*, 3(2), 166–185. https://doi.org/10.1093/workar/waw009

Uzialko, A. (2023, October 23). How to communicate with a multigenerational workforce. *Business News Daily*. https://www.businessnewsdaily.com/9708-multigenerational-workforce-communication.html#accommodating-the-whole-team

Villines, Z. (2022, April 19). Flow state: Definition, examples, and how to achieve it. *Medical News Today*. https://www.medicalnewstoday.com/articles/flow-state#:

Visual Objects. (2019, January 17). New survey by Visual Objects finds Generation Z dominates YouTube while other generations prefer

Facebook. *PR Newswire.* https://www.prnewswire.com/news-releases/
new-survey-by-visual-objects-finds-generation-z-dominates-youtube-
while-other-generations-prefer-facebook-300780361.html#:

W., E., & Suhail, T. (n.d.). How do you balance the use of digital and face-to-
face communication in your professional relationships? *LinkedIn.* https://
www.linkedin.com/advice/3/how-do-you-balance-use-digital-face-to-
face#know-your-context

What are behavioral metrics and how to track them in the app? (2022, May
25). *UserPilot Blog.* https://userpilot.com/blog/behavioral-metrics-saas/

What are the best ways to measure the success of your team's innovative and
creative efforts? (n.d.). *LinkedIn.* https://www.linkedin.com/advice/1/
what-best-ways-measure-success-your-teams

What is Gen Z? (2023, March 20). Mckinsey & Company. https://www.mckin
sey.com/featured-insights/mckinsey-explainers/what-is-gen-z

WhisperRoom. (2020, May 29). 7 benefits of silence: Why we need less noise.
https://whisperroom.com/tips/7-benefits-of-silence-why-we-need-less-
noise/#:

Why visual communication is important. (n.d.) *Eztalks.* https://eztalks.com/
unified-communications/why-visual-communication-is-important.html

Wicklethewait, J. (2023, November 20). Tackling Gen Z's social anxiety at
work with soft skills training. *Training Industry.* https://trainingindustry.
com/articles/performance-management/tackling-gen-zs-social-anxiety-
at-work-with-soft-skills-training/

Wilmes, M. (2022, March 31). Four generations, four styles of communication.
AnswerNet. https://answernet.com/blog-generations-styles-communica
tion/

Wong, K. (2020, September 22). Nine tips for building trust in the workplace.
Engage Blog. https://www.achievers.com/blog/building-trust-work
place/

Wooll, M. (2021, May 28). How to build trust in the workplace: Ten effective
solutions. *BetterUp.* https://www.betterup.com/blog/how-to-build-trust

Made in the USA
Monee, IL
08 December 2024

73038009R00098